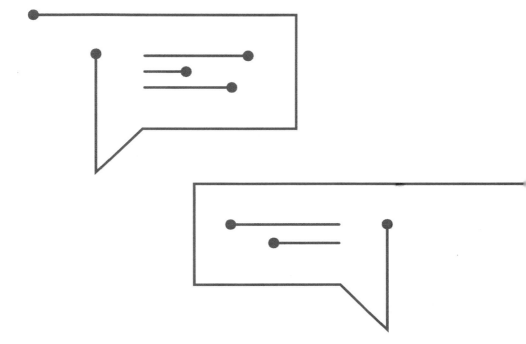

Digital Fluency

Building Success in the Digital Age

CHRISTIAN BRIGGS
& KEVIN MAKICE
ILLUSTRATED BY LARRY BUCHANAN

ISBN: 978-0-615-64294-9

Acknowlegements

We are indebted to many people who participated directly and indirectly in the research and writing of this book.

A first thanks goes to the team who worked on the initial research: Jenna McWilliams, Matt Snyder and Jay Steele. Without their creativity and patience with a challenging subject, this book would not have been possible. Thanks are also due to the ten organizations participating in that research. We have chosen not to use their names for case studies within the text, but their full and enthusiastic participation was invaluable.

We are thrilled to have Larry Buchanan involved in this project, lending his graphical genius to the book. Thanks also to Erin Wright for her willingness to help edit our words.

Along the way, many people have graciously spent time reading and critiquing drafts of the book in various states of readiness. In particular, thanks to Kate Haney, Louise and Bob Briggs, Simon Fowler, John Talbott, Mitch Coluzzi, Kristina Simacek, Esther Briggs, Ken Denmead, Joyce Kottra, Amy Makice and Maria O'Laughlin.

We would also like to thank the scholars, mentors and friends at Indiana University's School of Informatics and Computing who have taught us so much, and patiently guided us in the last half decade as we split our time between academic pursuits and building a company.

It is worth noting that Seymour Papert and Mitch Resnick developed an early concept of digital fluency two decades ago (Papert and Resnick, 1995), applicable to children's education. To our knowledge, digital fluency has not been introduced to broader organizational settings. We write this book not to replace Papert and Resnick's important work, but to extend it to a new audience.

Finally, we are so grateful to our families for their faithful patience with an, ahem, non-standard path through our academic and business pursuits. Amy, Carter, Archie and Matilda Makice and Esther Briggs—this is not possible without your continued support.

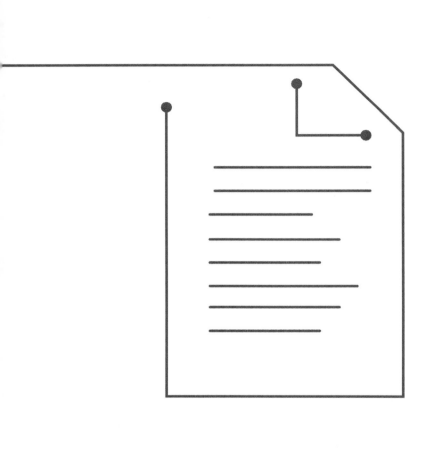

Table of Contents

Glossary

Ability — A person's capacity to affect the world.

Knowledge — Factual or procedural information that will help (or hinder) a person's actions.

Skill — Mental, verbal or physical manipulation of data or objects.

Mindset — A person's point of view on the world.

Anti-Literacy — The first of the four stages of fluency, characterized by rejection of the possibility that technology might have value.

Pre-Literacy — The second of the four stages of fluency, characterized by awareness of the potential value of using a technology, but an inability to use it.

Literacy — The third of the four stages of fluency, in which a person possesses basic abilities to use technology, but lacks understanding beyond its function.

Fluency — An ability to reliably achieve desired outcomes through use of technology.

Organization — Any group of people who arrange themselves and distribute tasks in service of a collective goal.

Digital Readiness — An organization's ability to create an optimal situation to support individual digital fluency.

Transparency — Operating in such a way that it is easy for others to see what actions are performed.

Social Network — A collection of relationships between actors that form a complex structure to carry information from one person to the next.

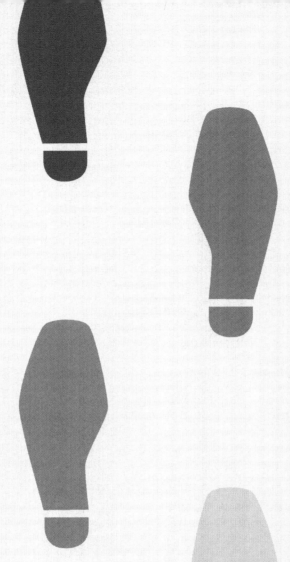

"Humans do not engage in activities that are meaningless. If you think you see people doing things you find meaningless, look again and try to understand what the activities mean for them."

—HENRY JENKINS

Slow Steps

On a warm evening at Davis Square in Somerville, Massachusetts, Samuel Smith walks up the stairs from the train station, ending his short ride home from work. Sam, 47, a consultant for a Boston firm that provides management education for companies, has a habit of walking too fast. Today, his steps are slower.

Sam is trying to figure something out. Over the course of the last few years, he has noticed large, slow-moving changes in his company. There are changes in his clients' companies, too. Previously, Sam had dismissed it as industry innovation, competitors trying to get a leg up or keep in pace with their customers. Today, however, he wonders if something bigger is happening.

Sam stops at a local bakery to pick up sugar cookies for his wife and two girls, who just 30 minutes ago had lobbied for the goodies via text message. Sam smiles at the memory, but still does not respond with his thumbs and the cell phone keypad. He hands a credit card to the cashier and looks forward to seeing three delighted faces when he gets home.

Stopping for anything is an unusual activity for Sam. Every day, his routine sees a little more work and a little less free time. His job often feels like triage, where he and his colleagues sift through projects hoping to save the most promising ones. Sam hears many complaints about how much time it takes to clear an email inbox and how that distracts from getting "real work" done.

He looks around the store at the other patrons. One young woman sits at a table sipping coffee and reading from a digital tablet. Behind her, a stack of fresh newspapers is undisturbed. Sam wonders if all of the iPads and Androids he sees explain why his clients seem to know more than he does about his business. Demand for the company newsletter, once considered a primary source for trends, has declined. Regularly, someone tells him how they heard the news first on Twitter.

With a bag of cookies in hand, Sam heads home with his uneasiness.

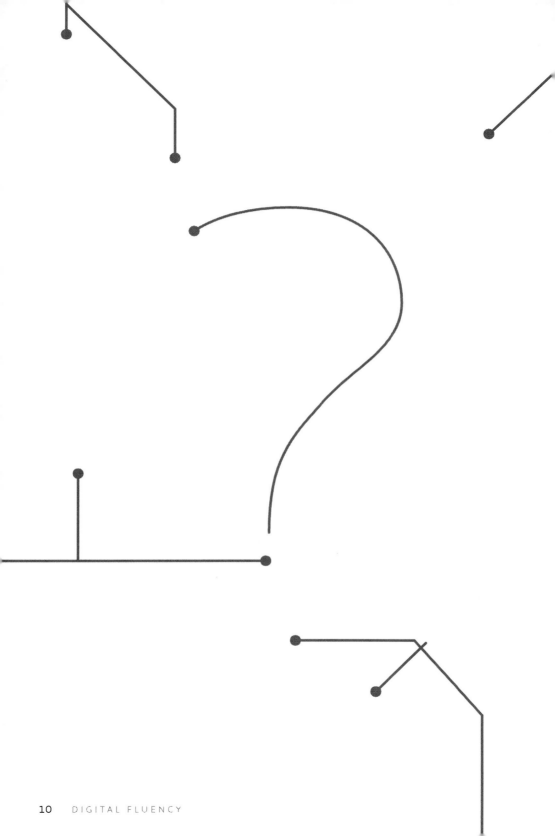

DIGITAL FLUENCY

Introduction

How this book can help you and your organization adapt to the digital age

Organizations today operate in an environment that is changing in ways and at a pace unprecedented in human history.

Internet-connected digital technology is widely available around the globe. Data is created by more authors and available to more consumers than ever before. Customers, employees, managers and leaders—highly connected to one another inside and outside of the workplace—have access to powerful communication and coordination technologies which enable them to do both great service and great harm. Cultural norms of sharing, transparency, propriety, humor, satire and identity are shifting, as are business practices. Collaboration happens easily outside of the purview of formal leadership. New businesses are born quickly, but there are more ways than ever for an organization to contribute to its own demise.

All of these changes create unique opportunities to innovate, but also pose fundamental challenges to the way that we have lived, worked, socialized and managed organizations and institutions for so long[1].

As everyone wrestles with this reality, one vital question frequently comes to mind:

1
Gary Hamel points out that "..the foundations of 'modern' management were laid by people like Daniel McCallum, Frederick Taylor, and Henry Ford, all of whom were born before the end of the American Civil War in 1865." [Hamel, 2009]

How can we adapt and help ourselves succeed in the digital age?

This book was written to help you answer this question by working through the hopes, questions and fears behind it, and moving toward strategic use of digital tools. We can begin to answer that big question by first paying attention to the smaller, more specific questions it encompasses.

How much needs to change?
Success is achieved through a combination of improving your abilities and adjusting how your organization operates. The levers you pull must steer your organization toward the waves of change without getting swamped. You might replace the software used to reach out to customers while leaving the organizational structure intact. New job roles may become necessary, or hiring practices may require an overhaul. To successfully adapt, you must understand what is within your power to change and what impact those actions might have on the organization.

What should be changed first?
Once you identify the things that need to change, consider their priority and dependencies. Every day, something different will demand your attention. Choosing where to start may impact how well future efforts are implemented. New communication and collaboration tools could be doomed to fail without adjustments to policies and procedures. Without active participation from the leadership, operational employees may be reluctant to adopt new tools and procedures. It may be important to re-work an organizational structure to become more agile prior to offering employee training. Making decisions that focus on improving the wrong thing may undermine your efforts to improve.

How does the context of an organization impact decisions?
A shoe retailer is a different kind of business than a tractor

manufacturer, and both are different from a non-profit charity. The differences in how these organizations are structured may necessitate distinct approaches to the challenges and benefits of the digital age.

The manufacture of heavy equipment might benefit most from efficiencies that networked people and information bring, whereas a small business in a local market might focus on empowering loyal customers to augment what the company can do with limited resources. For highly-regulated industries, like finance or medical devices, there is a new set of obstacles to the use of digital media, courtesy of protective protocols and strategic needs for security. These constraints do not mean these industries are insulated from change, but how they adapt must account for the rules and norms under which they operate.

> Not everything needs to change in order for an organization to thrive in the digital age.

The answers to these important questions are not easy, but they do contain good news. First, not everything needs to change in order for an organization to thrive in the digital age. Second, there are recognizable patterns emerging to guide organizations toward effective adaptation within its particular context[2].

No matter what your particular organization's answers are to the previous three questions, a key part of the solution must involve *digital fluency*—the maximum potential an individual has to achieve desired outcomes through the use of digital technology. Fluency is the result of individuals continuing to maintain and improve skills relative to the needs of your organizational context. Your fluency helps you act in a way that anticipates and supports change.

2
SociaLens is currently conducting extensive research to better understand these patterns. Our next book will report on these findings.

To preface this important topic, we first take a step back to look at the digital age historically. Although the question of how an organization can succeed in the digital age appears to be new, its answer is derived from an old truth: Humans communicate and organize.

The evolution of technology continually provides opportunities to direct communication through new channels.

Uniquely, we humans rely heavily on the combination of signs (e.g., gestures, sounds, and alphabets) and media technologies (e.g., pen and paper, radio, telephones, and the Internet) to connect us. Once connected, we can collaborate or fight with each other, develop love or foster hatred, bring countries together or tear them apart. We have a long history of doing this, even as the available technology has changed:

The ancient Greeks shared information through epic poetry about themselves, preserved in writing for future generations.

Abraham Lincoln used the telegraph in the U.S. Civil War to receive real-time updates and send commands to his army generals.

In 1944, husbands and wives separated by war used handwritten letters and an international postal system to stay connected across oceans.

Two generations ago, an unemployed person looking for a job contacted employers with typed applications and phone calls, responding to suitable want ads published in newspapers.

The evolution of technology continually provides opportunities to direct communication through new channels, but the motivation to communicate is largely unchanged.

Cable provider Comcast famously used Twitter in 2008 as a way to connect with customers in real-time and reverse their poor service reputation[3]. Since 2009, political protesters around the world routinely make use of Internet-enabled mobile devices to communicate their grievances and coordinate their actions. Technology has altered their potential for success and the kinds of outcomes they can hope to achieve.

With each successive generation, a need arises for new abilities which continue to allow people to connect with each other effectively. Some transitions, like going from snail mail to using email, require different knowledge, skills and mindsets. A person who is able only to create and send marketing material and persuasive business proposals by postal mail might be mystified by a modern email client. Understanding the etiquette of email, its effectiveness for broadcasting messages, and how to manage group lists helps that person master this new technology.

Other transitions, such as moving from a land line telephone to a cell phone, require slight adjustments. For a person who can dial numbers and hold conversations via a land line telephone, the ability to use a cell phone is not difficult to develop, but it includes knowing when the pervasive access to friends and customers becomes abuse. A person's potential for success with these transitions depends on their ability to align the new circumstance with their current goals.

Ability alone is not enough, however. Other factors—including policies, available resources, and feedback about progress—play a critical role in both defining and achieving success. In our early work with organizations

3
Frank Eliason began using Twitter to find disgruntled customers and initiate an online conversation. By being proactive and open about troubleshooting, Comcast became social media darlings. Eliason left the company in 2010, but his technique remains a model for engagement.

that were attempting to deal with a major change, we found many examples of people who should have been able to adapt to digital technologies, but struggled to do so.

In one large IT consulting organization, we met a person who was tech-savvy—a quality many would assume guarantees successful use of digital media—and comfortable using social media. As he moved up through the ranks to become a director of 700 employees, this MIT graduate had stopped using those tools in the company.

In a leadership training company, we encountered well-educated, gregarious storytellers—communication skills that should lead to digital success—whose use of an internal collaboration platform could not gain sufficient traction. This failure to adopt came despite the CEO's complete financial and verbal support.

Restrictive legal policies, time pressures, detached leadership, and other organizational circumstances contributed to their difficulty. These people thought the transition from using tools like Microsoft Office and company Intranets to business applications of social networks, blogs, microblogs, and wikis should be an easy one. Although all of these tools are largely run on exactly the same computer systems, the abilities that a person needs in order to use them well are quite different. Without these abilities, success remains elusive.

This book is about that transition and the personal journey to develop sufficient ability—what we call *digital fluency*—needed to thrive in this digital age.

In **Chapter 1** ("A Changed World"), we examine the speed and complexity evident in the world today. We discuss the ways this change affects how we handle information, interact, involve and inspire other people, and innovate and imagine the future.

In **Chapter 2** ("Embracing Change"), we help to answer the question of how ready you might be for the digital age. This preparation is described as three contributors to your abilities: knowledge, skills and mindset.

In **Chapter 3** ("Becoming Fluent"), we explore the four learning stages we go through to develop digital fluency, emphasizing the importance of continually striving to be fluent. Because the world continues to change, so must you.

In **Chapter 4** ("Success In Context"), we give a quick overview of how organizations can achieve *digital readiness*, the means of supporting employee digital fluency by aligning resources, culture, and purpose with the tasks those employees are asked to undertake. We also explore how to define and measure success.

Finally in **Chapter 5** ("Starting Today"), we suggest some specific activities and exercises that you can undertake to embrace the new normal of digital change.

Throughout this book, we will also illustrate the core concepts of digital fluency through the story of two characters, Sam and Louise, based on real people we observed during the last two years. We follow their respective journeys toward digital fluency, concluding these vignettes with a glimpse into a future where they are fluent people in digitally ready organizations.

Digital fluency is an important topic. It is valuable for organizations to know what it is, how it compares with other fluencies, and how it is useful to achieving strategic success.

A Few Things You Should Know About This Book

Though the main focus of this book is an individual's journey through the learning process of digital fluency, most of the content and concepts are explained as a journey occurring within and affecting the *organizational* context.

The insights in this book have emerged from three major sources:

- Rapid ethnography[4] and interviews conducted in 10 organizations. We have altered or omitted the names of the people and organizations in order to focus on the truths evident in each case, some of which show hard lessons for the participant organizations.

- Academic research in the areas of media theory, organizational and management theory, institutional theory, psychology and human-computer interaction.

- Personal experiences over the last two decades working in and around organizations of all shapes and sizes as employees, managers, consultants and trainers.

We hope you will keep in mind that our motivation for writing this book is not to provide an exhaustive theoretical argument or conduct an academic debate on the ontological nature of digital fluency. Rather, our goal is to help you make sense of and better thrive in a complex digital world.

Although there is much peer-reviewed research behind the ideas contained in these pages, we have tried to forego the

4
Rapid ethnography is a collection of field methods (observation, participation, interviews) intended to provide a reasonable understanding of people and their activities in a particular context, such as an office. Unlike real ethnography, there are significant time and resource constraints that limit time in the field.

academic arguments in favor of practical examples. Our intent is to provide information useful to use when talking to colleagues about succeeding in the digital age. For readers wanting to delve into the academic arguments, we provide a rich resource list at the end of this book.

Want to find out how digitally fluent you are?

Take a short survey at mydigitalfluency.socialens.com to find out.

"The death of distance will probably be the single most important economic force shaping society in the first half of this century. Its effects will be as pervasive as those of the discovery of electricity."

—FRANCES CAIRNCROSS

The Handshake Deal

Louise Johnson is lost in thought as she walks down the city sidewalk, barely noticing the man with the bakery bag until he adeptly moves to avoid collision. Louise, 55, notices the clamshell phone open in his hand and wonders why people spend so much time with those things. *We are turning into a bunch of antisocial misfits*, she thinks.

She is on her way home from work at Superior Machinery, a precision manufacturing business she started with her husband in 1982. The company grew to 70 employees before her husband died, leaving Louise to run it on her own these past four years. Business is good, but she is worried about the future. She doesn't want to rock the boat by investing in new computer software when the current tools are adequate. Her confidence wanes with every step.

A talented, self-taught machinist and now CEO, Louise carries the business section of *The Boston Globe* under her arm. She is always looking for competitive advantages that will make her business more effective. Today's articles are the same as last week's, declaring a need for businesses to "adopt social media" and to use it to "listen to their customers." Louise is skeptical this will work for her business. Deals are made with a verbal conversation and a hand shake. You can't replace the personal touch, right?

The city streets are bustling, but Louise can't find an available cab. As she waves at another one, Louise is crafting a new memo in her mind, one that will keep "social media" away from her worker bees. She knows the stories about predators, the online rumor mill, and loss of productivity. She's afraid some employee is going to leak privileged information and trade secrets to competitors online. Maybe having her IT director block MySpace and Facebook will keep those problems out of her company. He's young, so he'll know what to do.

Thunder booms somewhere in the distance. Louise didn't bring an umbrella, but has her *Globe* ready if the rain starts before she finds a cab home.

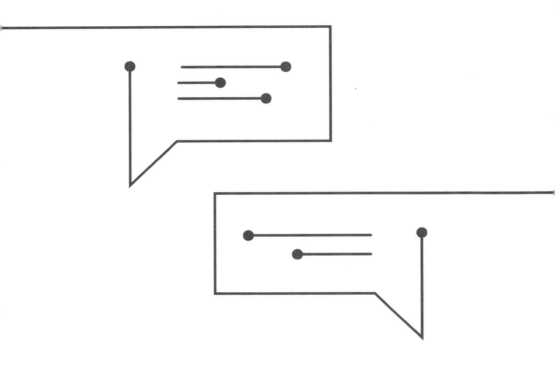

1

A Changed World

Speed and complexity affect the way we think, what we know, and what we do

Ours is an era of speed. The magnitude and pace of change in the world is increasing daily.

As James Burke once said:

> "...[I]t took centuries for information about the smelting of ore to cross a single continent and bring about the Iron Age. During the time of sailing ships, it took years for that which was known to become that which was shared.
>
> When man stepped onto the moon, it was known and seen in every corner of the globe 1.4 seconds later—and that is hopelessly slow by today's standards [Hock, 2000]."

Burke's statement was made prior to the existence of the major social media tools of the past decade, such as MySpace, YouTube, Facebook, and Twitter. Whatever the standard to which he referred at the time, the game has changed dramatically in the years since. Digital technology is a critical part of this escalating change, and electricity is at its core[1].

1
The media theorist Marshall McLuhan claimed that electricity "ended sequence by making things instant" [McLuhan, 1964].

Digital is Different

For thousands of years, the speed of communication and innovation increased incrementally, as additional channels became available and were slowly adopted around the world.

> **For the first time in history, communication dramatically diminished the limiting effects of geography.**

In the 19th century, society harnessed and propagated electricity as a new source of energy, giving us the ability to encode and send messages instantly across long distances. For the first time in history, communication—a vital component of change—dramatically diminished the limiting effects of geography, effectively compressing time for those who no longer needed to invest months traveling around the world for a conversation. Change could happen more rapidly, at greater distances, and with less perceived cost.

Since then, the pace of change has steadily increased, with widespread effects on what we know, what we can do, and our understanding of the way the world works[2]. Companies launch and shut down in rapid cycles. A single report can threaten entire industries with extinction. Political action is coordinated faster than mainstream news can report. Anyone from a huge multinational corporation to a teenager with a cell phone can spread information.

Media theorist Marshall McLuhan and others have referred to this phenomenon as "electric speed" [Johnson, 1999]: Not only does speed make it difficult to predict how a market, or a society might change, but when a change does occur, it can strike like lightning.

[2]
As David Pace, an Indiana University history professor, put it: "I can't think of another time in history where we've had to re-educate an entire generation so many times."

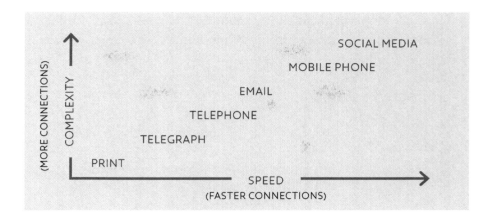

Figure 1.1
The increasing
speed and
complexity of
the digital age

Ours is also an era of complexity. Each part of our network of people and machines is highly connected to the others, affecting each other in ways that are increasingly difficult to predict. Children can send text messages to their parents from school that express love, ask for a ride home, or convey instant reaction to a tough test. Customers can connect with a CEO through their shared social networks to express gratitude or dissatisfaction. Financial markets, closely integrated through technology, can change the behavior of investors, who react instantly on one side of the world to economic upheaval on the other.

Coupled with the increased speed[3] (see Figure 1.1), this level of connectivity tends to produce unpredictable situations that defy conventional strategies. Even the US Army significantly altered their operating procedures in the face of what they call "... growing uncertainty, rapid change, increased competitiveness, and greater decentralization" [US Army, 2009].

Complexity often brings positive results. Paul Smith, a former radio presenter, used his Twitter network to hitchhike halfway around the globe[4], from the UK to the shores of New Zealand, all on the kindness of strangers [Smith, 2010]. Texas roommates Jamie Whitt and Connie Donnellan found an injured pitbull in need of immediate

3
Think of speed as the time it takes for change to occur, and complexity as the difficulty of predicting the result of a chain of effects. By most accounts both have generally increased in the digital age.

4
Smith made his "twitchhiker" trip in just 30 days, establishing some rules to make the challenge difficult. He could not: pay for any transport or accommodation himself, plan anything more than three days in advance, spend longer than 48 hours in any one location, solicit any offers of help, or accept help from people not using Twitter.

care, including amputations. Under the threat of the wounded animal's euthanasia , the two women appealed to their social network and quickly raised the money needed to save the dog [Parr, 2009].

> Unexpected value often comes from the mundane.

Complexity leads to negative results, too. In 2009, an employee of United Airlines broke musician Dave Carroll's guitar. After attempting to work with the company's customer service, Carroll sent an email to United [Carroll, 2009] stating that he would be:

> *"... writing three songs about United Airlines and my experience in the whole matter. I would then make videos for these songs and share them on YouTube, inviting viewers to vote on their favourite United song. My goal: to get one million hits in one year."*

In a less complex world, a small-time musician writing a song would not impact a large organization like United. In just a few weeks, however, Carroll's first video, "United Breaks Guitars," gained over 4 million views on YouTube[5]. Although the connection is anecdotal, United's stock dropped 10 percent within four days of its launch [Financial Times, 2009].

Unexpected value often comes from the mundane. One man, after paying a pricey $1,200 repair bill from his local auto shop, posted the following to his Twitter feed with no goal other than making a joke:

> *"Nissan mechanic said that the ECM on my car went kaput like a computer processor. Knew I shouldn't have kept running Windows 98."*

Within an hour, a friend living 1,000 miles away replied

[5] Highly-connected communities continued to forwarded the video to one another. Two years later, the video accumulated nearly 11 million views.

Speed and complexity affect how we:

- Find, filter, and use knowledge from a variety of trusted sources
- Critically choose an identity (or identities) to engage with others through multiple channels
- Motivate people to act in support of common goals
- Make people aware of the current situation and empower them to apply their strengths toward an organizational need
- Help others to understand what is likely to happen and possible to do in a future situation
- Critically reflect on past situations to creatively imagine new ideas, then act decisively to make those ideas a reality

both with empathy about the car troubles and with information about how to get the money back from the dealer, who had been unaware of a manufacturer's recall for the defective part. This unexpected message from an unexpected source yielded unexpected results and saved him $1,200.

It is natural to hesitate when faced with injecting new tools into an established routine. Doing so usually requires an investment of time and money to investigate their benefit, let alone to successfully implement that technology into existing business processes. There are certainly situations where tools do not fit an organizational need and adopting them is detrimental. However, rejecting the digital tools as a means of mitigating change[6] without deeply considering possible value—particularly through hands-on experimentation— is like refusing to eat because the chef has changed.

In order to achieve success in this increasingly speedy, complex world (see Table 1.1), the ways we do things must change. We will explore these changes in the remainder of this chapter.

Table 1.1
The effects
of speed and
complexity

6
According to Angela Ahrendts, the CEO of Burberry's: "You have to create a Social Enterprise today. You have to. If you don't do that, I don't know what your business model is in 5 years." The British luxury store, founded in 1856, currently boasts over 500 stores in 50 countries.

Handling Information

We are in the midst of a decades-old shift from information scarcity to information abundance. As this information abundance increases, we need to change not only the ways we find and filter information, but also how we create, evaluate, transform, store, and share it with other people.

In 2010, an Internet story broke about a woman who quit her job by communicating her displeasure with her sexist boss through a series of photos of her with a dry-erase whiteboard (see Figure 1.2). Within hours, the story had reached well-known publications like *Fast Company*, who initially presented the incident as factual.

However, some had doubts. One member of the extended SociaLens digital network posted the following message on Twitter:

> *"OK, the girl resigning via dry-erase board is a good story, but the skeptic in me wonders how many minutes till we find out that's fake"*

The author's Twitter update provided clues to his ability to effectively handle digital information. First, though he has a full-time job, he heard about the story soon after it had occurred. This suggests some skill at monitoring external information and multitasking. Second, his skepticism shows a learned sense of what authenticity looks like on the Internet. "The woman seemed 'too perfect,'" he told us. "Like she'd been sought out for the role."

The author credited past experiences with information on the Internet—including the "Balloon Boy" coverage, where a young boy had reportedly climbed aboard a homemade balloon[7]—in honing his skills.

The ability to filter for authenticity has increased in importance due to the amount of data streaming into one's life. When the volume of that stream exceeds the ability to deal with it, we call this *information overload*, a phenomenon which is clearly having a huge effect on organizations [Spira, 2011; Toffler, 1970; Simon, 1963] by blurring work and personal time, increasing stress, and undermining group dynamics with miscommunication.

If someone experiences more information than makes sense, the result is increased stress, confusion, and a tendency for mistakes such as forwarding incorrect information to others. When mistakes happen with digital media, high quantities of irrelevant information can be propagated to other people, generating more overload.

Individuals need to understand where the value resides in the massive amounts of information flowing into our lives each day. This understanding allows a fluent person to make appropriate and effective use of what they find across multiple channels and reflects a significant change in today's information world.

7
This 2009 story proved false, but for several hours captivated social and traditional media alike as the balloon was tracked on its 50-mile journey. Falcon Heene, 6, was never on board, in a hoax perpetuated by his parents to gain publicity for a reality show.

Information overload

At least three different forms of information overload have emerged from our research and conversations with people:

1. The Firehose

More information surfaces than a person can physically or mentally process. This can result in job stress and a resistance to trying new tools or procedures, for fear of getting further behind. The Firehose often happens after significant changes in personnel, digital systems, or internal policy.

2. The Haystack

The quantity of information can create a nagging sense that a person has missed something important, but identifying that key message is like finding a needle in a haystack. This form of overload usually comes after experiencing the Firehose for a while, as a person tries to deal with how to filter the information to make it useful. Haystacks can result in redundant scanning of content in the hope of rediscovering some lost piece of information.

3. The Sinbox

One method of dealing with information overload is to ignore the bulk of unprocessed content and start anew. Doing so can create anxiety over the unread emails or other ignored messages. This feeling also shows up when other work prevents dealing with incoming messages. The result of Sinbox is distraction from what is happening in the moment, or a shorter attention span as one's thoughts constantly return to the information queue.

Interacting With People

There is a common perception that use of the Internet decreases the number of face-to-face social interactions people have. This is most often not the case. Offline social interactions are commonly mixed with those online. Establishing and managing one's identity in these changing contexts is an important, yet challenging, task.

The explosion of digital channels by which we mediate our relationships makes it necessary for us to critically craft and gain confidence in the ways we present ourselves. In some situations, it may be appropriate to create a different identity for each community. In other cases, one identity is used in all contexts.

Navigating the blurry line between personal and professional roles is a struggle for many people. It is a common presumption that a clear separation must exist, but a fluent person will consider a variety of responses to:

> *Should a CEO use the same Facebook or Twitter account that she uses for sharing personal thoughts?*

> *Should my profile picture be a highly-produced professional photo, or a picture with my kids?*

> *What voice should be used when writing for a professional organization?*

The answers depend on context. Tony Hsieh, CEO of Zappos, for example, is clearly comfortable using social media both as an official corporate communication channel, and as a way to share personal information. That doesn't work well for every executive. Ultimately, a person's ability to interact with other people is most affected by how comfortable she feels with her decisions.

Inspiring Other People

The ways we motivate others to action must also adapt to the digital age. Consider the case of a global consulting firm, whose CEO was a strong advocate for his organization's use of digital media as a collaborative tool.

The employees—an intelligent, talkative group who were already willing to collaborate offline—exhibited a low rate of adoption of these tools and practices. Despite encouragement from the well-respected leader and a significant allocation of resources to support integration with existing systems, these bright, capable people were slow to change. The explanation is not intuitive.

For two decades, this company cultivated a collaborative, open culture. During that time, top-down rules dictated only a small percentage of employee actions; behavior was primarily modeled by senior executives. In this culture— or perhaps because of it—the CEO had become the moral leader of the organization. While he asked for and openly supported the adoption of digital collaboration tools, he *did not use them himself.* Failure to model the new behavior doomed the initiative[8].

This CEO failed to understand that the use of digital collaboration tools is a highly social yet vulnerable activity for many people. Users of such tools perform before an audience of friends, colleagues, and even strangers [Bardzell, Bolter, Löwgren, 2010]. This is a big change from older forms of computer software and hardware that were primarily used alone or to simply to mediate relationships in a one-to-one fashion.

Getting employees to adopt new applications is like dancing at the annual holiday party. Most people will not shake their tailfeathers until the boss gets out on

8
In a norms-based culture, people do things to satisfy social norms. In a rules-based culture, they do things in order to gain formal reward or to avoid formal sanctions.

the dance floor. Unless the top-level folks model digital collaboration in a public manner, it will be extremely difficult to create a norm which makes it acceptable for employees to follow suit.

Inspiration goes beyond getting people to use technology. The overall motivations and personal priorities of employees are changing as well.

> Only one in nine employees are emotionally connected to their workplaces.

In a 2011 research study of 2,800 college students and recent college grads, one in three participants responded that they value social media freedom, device flexibility, and work mobility over salary when accepting a job offer. Two-thirds of the college students would choose an Internet connection over a car [Cisco Systems, 2011].

Many people aren't inspired at all by their organizations. Recent research found that only about "one in nine employees worldwide are emotionally connected to their workplaces and feel they have the resources and support they need to succeed" [Gallup, 2011].

These trends are an indication that the increasing use of digital technology is deeply connected to keeping people engaged in their work and with each other. Increasingly so in times of economic stress, employees are aware of good work environments, as evaluated by a range of qualitative metrics that include flexible time, freedom of expression, and depth of feedback on their own progress.

In order to succeed, we all need to understand what motivates the people around us, and how to contribute to an environment where those personal priorities are honored, powering the efforts that yield positive results for everyone involved.

Involving Other People

Few people will recognize the name Isaiah Mustafa, but most recognize the character he famously portrays: the Old Spice Man[9]. Much of the early credit for the award-winning advertising campaign—revitalizing a stodgy brand of men's aftershave products—was directed toward the marketing firm that orchestrated the outreach, Wieden+Kennedy [Leporte, 2010].

As the first ad was released, Wieden+Kennedy augmented their own talent pool by luring experienced digital media producer Iain Tait to become Global Interactive Executive Creative Director [Morrissey, 2010]. That hire was one part of an organizational chain—from a trusting client (Procter & Gamble) down to the fluent specialists who crafted the content—that found ways to match individual strengths to the task at hand. Success was a byproduct of involvement.

In July 2010, Tait's team embarked on a risky project: the Old Spice Man would respond in real time to people engaging the brand online. For two long days, a group of writers, videographers, and digital media specialists joined Mustafa on the set to reintroduce the popular character to specific communities. Using a custom application, the team scanned the Internet across multiple social media platforms and blogs to find messages with creative and influential appeal [Borden, 2010]. With each custom video response, a new link passed around the Internet generated thousands of new tweets and comments.

Within 24 hours, the team accumulated 181 video replies posted to YouTube, receiving 6.7 million views [Wiancko, 2010]. By comparison, the original commercial released in early February took five months to get to 13 million views

9
The "Smell Like a Man, Man" campaign kicked off in February 2010 as a clever series of television and Internet advertisements featuring an ideal man (Mustafa) doing and saying all of the things his special someone would want him to do and say.

[YouTube, 2010]. The short, real-time videos became social objects that people willingly shared with family and friends, creating value that lasted well beyond the two-day investment of resources[10]. That value extended further when flattering imitations appeared, using the cultural language of the ad to promote other causes[11].

After the completion of their innovative project, Tait lauded P&G's role in the success of the video campaign:

> *"Without a client brave enough to work in this kind of compressed time frame again there would be nothing. That relationship of trust and understanding has been built up over time by a team of people working here at W+K and P&G, turning out great work and learning from it each step of the way"* [Tait, 2010].

The agency and client worked under a set of principles they agreed would guide the video production, but Proctor & Gamble decided to de-emphasize the traditional sign-offs and legal approval, allowing the campaign to operate in real time[12]. As Tait told *Fast Company*, "They know that because we love this thing, we're not going to be irresponsible with it and throw it away and lose the chance to do it again" [Borden, 2010].

Thriving in the digital age requires us to look beyond the job titles scaffolding an organizational chart to find people with skills to fill needed roles. Those skills then need to be nurtured through resources and policies that empower people to do good work.

10
The business impact of this campaign was concrete: Sales went up 7 percent in the year Mustafa became the Old Spice spokesman [Zaidi, 2010], including jumps of 55 percent in May to July and a whopping 107 percent in the month following the YouTube campaign [Parpis, 2010].

11
For examle, immediately following the Old Spice success, Brigham Young University's Harold B. Lee Library released a tribute parody encouraging students to go to the library and improve their grades [Careaga, 2010].

12
W+K didn't always have this kind of support. Just three years earlier, the agency briefly lost about 15 percent of their Nike contract [NY Times, 2007] due to inexperience with digital strategy. They corrected that by hiring expertise and developing their fluency [Morrissey, 2008]. Tait was one of those adjustments.

Innovating

The increased speed and complexity of digital media makes effective innovation more critical than ever. Better tools and connectivity between collaborators facilitate innovation, but the rapid pace of change also increases the need for it.

Three mutually dependent things comprise innovation:

1. *Critical Reflection*—reframing problems by questioning assumptions about data and situations.

2. *Creative Thinking*—generating not-yet-proven ideas to transform the current situation into a future one.

3. *Effective Implementation*—turning creative ideas into practical reality in ways that perpetuate the innovation cycle (e.g., future ideation).

Digital media is surprisingly innovative when considered in these terms. Even the simple act of posting a 140-character message on Twitter is rife with opportunities to try new things for improving practice.

The default call to action on Twitter is a simple question: *What's happening?* That prompt may seem trivial, but those few words paralyze many with the possible interpretations and consequences from answering it. What is posted in response could be seen by anyone following the account, including those beyond one's own network. This is true even if the post is later deleted (such is the nature of the Internet). It is important, therefore, for a person to be able to cycle through the three parts of innovation quickly, trying out and evaluating possible actions in their head before typing a single character.

Someone with a strong ability to innovate will quickly consider the context of the people who might read a post. Being sensitive to their personal joys and sorrows can influence how a message is *conceived*. Experience evolves one's expectations of what is considered suitable etiquette or appropriate content.

The able Twitterer will also realize that contributing to the information stream of others is only half of engagement. The other half is listening, monitoring for responses and relevant information that could change how a message is *perceived*. Each time a question is answered—Did people respond to the post favorably? Was it passed along to others outside the poster's network?—positive experiences lessen any hesitancy to share new ideas with the world.

From our earlier case study—the leadership training company failing to gain traction for an internal collaboration platform—the intelligent and gregarious employees also suffered from perfectionism. Many individuals lacked the ability to innovate because they sought to produce content that was either precisely worded or deeply vetted. One person had a pragmatic sign over his desk that read "80 percent is good enough" to remind him to push projects out the door.

In the innovation cycle, they were stuck on reflection, identifying so many potential missteps they could not generate new ideas, and avoiding implementation in order to avoid failure. Even with just 140 characters to use on Twitter, that fear of flawed content is often big enough to inhibit sharing.

When people have the confidence to innovate, digital media can be used to improve one's knowledge, skills and mindset. In turn, organizations leverage the abilities that result from innovation to adapt to a new situation.

Innovation In Action

Innovation is a cycle of experimentation and reflection that is critical for sustaining organizational success. No startup business ever survived by sticking with their initial idea, and rare is the established company that can outlast changes to the customer experience without making adjustments.

To support an innovative culture within an organization does not require massive shifts in business plans or a great investment of resources. Some things are quite simple, yet effective:

Sockington

In 2007, Jason Scott set his cat, Sockington, up with a Twitter account. As his pet's proxy, Scott tweeted observations from the feline perspective. Socks gained a steady following and, after Twitter added the account to the featured users list, skyrocketed to 1.5 million followers. The most famous cat on Twitter has since expanded to other forms of digital media, with Scott selling t-shirts and making plans for a book. Socks Army was spawned to promote charities and causes benefiting animals.

Jesse's Blend

In 2009, a local gourmet food store held an online contest to suggest a new type of coffee blend. Customers voted for their favorite submission, and "Jesse's Blend" was turned into a real product for the store. The coffee sold quite well, and is still on the shelf years later.

Creative Music

At a large public university, a creative services department recently underwent an organizational overhaul, shuffling personnel and changing their business model. As part of their ongoing efforts to change their culture, one of the directors solicited favorite songs to see a Pandora Internet radio station. The result was an ecclectic mix of musical tastes that helped create a shared experience for the team of two dozen diverse staffers.

Imagining the Future

The questions most often asked by those who reject digital technology is, "What is its return on investment?" While you may find a number of simple answers through Google, ROI is not a straightforward calculation. It involves as many qualitative measures as quantitative ones, and depends heavily on the current context.

For an organization new to digital media, the real struggle is to imagine the *future* value of these tools. Initially, this may be limited to financial metrics, like the number of additional sales. The more digitally fluent a person becomes, the more quickly he will be able to imagine wider definitions of value, extending benefits by also considering three key factors:

1. The intangible benefits arising from use of digital media (e.g., psychological)

2. The level of investment required (e.g., skills training)

3. The ways to measure success (e.g., happy customers)

Each depends on the ability to rapidly gather information, to experiment, and to involve other people in the process—actions previously discussed in this chapter.

Understanding what to expect from a tool is critical to success. However, it is easier to imagine a possible future benefit from using a tool if one also understands its limitations and barriers to adoption. Hands-on experience can bring these insights into focus, much like test driving a car will reveal to a potential customer how the vehicle sounds, smells, and responds on the road. An organization probably won't fully understand what is involved without decision-makers diving in first.

Ultimately, imagining a future—to envision what is likely to happen and possible to do in a future situation—is only valuable if it leads to change. Imagination also requires communication and persuasion, in order to help others grasp the shared goals and responsibilities necessary to make them a reality.

Digital technology can be used to imagine the broader future in new ways. In 2007, the massive online Alternate Reality Game[13] *World Without Oil* was launched. The game simulated a 32-week global energy crisis. 1,500 participants created and uploaded video and audio recordings, photos, text and art, depicting their lives and the world around them without oil. 68,000 people participated in the game as consumers of that original content [World Without Oil].

Digital tools help with organizational needs, too. A recent example comes from the Wikimedia Foundation. Using that organizations's online platform, over 1,000 people using 50 different languages co-authored a five-year strategic plan for the Foundation in a twelve-month period [WikiMedia, 2011].

13
An Alternate Reality Game (ARG) is an interactive game with an evolving narrative overlaying onto the real world. Fictional stories are used as a platform for puzzles, group activities, and information that is hidden across multiple forms of media, including traditional media (e.g., newspapers) and physical objects.

Many of the things we do in organizations—dealing with information, interacting with, inspiring and involving other people, innovating and imagining the future—constitute a powerful engine of success, propelling us forward to achieve significant goals. The digital age has altered how we are able to take these actions and how quickly we must act. Each change feeds the next. If you are now wondering, "Am I ready for the change?" (the topic of the next chapter), the good news is you and your organization may be more ready than you think.

Rewind

What we've covered so far

Electric speed is a phenomenon owing to digital information, allowing us to communicate instantly across great distances.

People and their devices are linked together in a complex network that leads to unpredictable outcomes.

Even the mundane can generate value.

If someone experiences more information than makes sense— *information overload*—the result is increased stress, confusion, and a tendency to make mistakes.

A person's ability to interact with other people is most affected by how comfortable she feels with her decisions.

The motivations and personal priorities of employees are changing.

Skills need to be nurtured through resources and policies that empower people to do good work.

Innovation is a cycle of reflection, creative thinking, and implementation.

Imagination requires communication and persuasion to help turn shared goals into reality.

"The qualities that make Twitter seem inane
and half-baked are what makes it so powerful."

—JONATHAN ZITTRAIN

Poetry is Back

Sam remembers his first big mistake on Twitter. It wasn't costly, but it still shakes him up when he thinks about it.

At his daughter's urging several months earlier, Sam joined Twitter to stay connected with her. After a few weeks of reading her "tweets," he discovered some co-workers were using Twitter, too. Sam recalls his decision to start sharing things he was doing at work. Once, he had posted while on a business trip: "Just arrived at the client site. Heading in."

Although the information is harmless by itself, Sam now realizes that he had enabled his smartphone's ability to share his current location with each message. It was easy to tell who his client was that day. That extra information is potentially a breech of confidentiality, a disastrous mistake for Sam and his company.

Sam thinks about that incident as he pages through a thick book about using Twitter. He is amazed at all the jargon—network effects, transparency, meme, and hashtag—that seemed so revolutionary when he first picked the book up at the local bookstore. He recalls setting the book back down on the store shelf, fearing he wasn't ready to cast aside his familiar old world for this new one he didn't fully understand.

Now, Sam notices something interesting: many activities and skills from that old world are still needed, even with everyone using Twitter. In fact, he is rediscovering old skills, like writing poetry and moderating town hall meetings. The faster this new world gets, the more human connections resemble the neighborhoods where his grandfather grew up.

Sitting in the lobby of his current client's office, Sam pages through the book he plans to lend to a sales manager. In addition to the techie vocabulary, the book is great for changing one's perception of the tool. He closes the book, and pulls out his smartphone to tweet: "New doesn't seem as scary as it once did." Location awareness is already disabled.

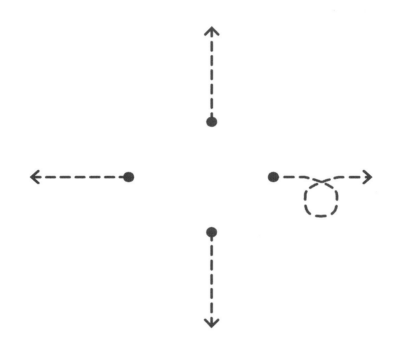

2

Embracing Change

You may be more ready than you think

Joe is a man with an endearing smile and a jovial laugh. He was also a Vice President in charge of a communications group for a large organization. More than twice as old as the World Wide Web, Joe didn't use digital media. He saw the tools as something that other, mostly younger, people used when they wanted to share too much information. When asked if he could ever join them, Joe replied:

> *"No, I'm not ever going to develop those skills. It's a cultural thing. I will be the last person in America on Facebook."*

Joe felt as though he was never going to be ready for such a change, and he's not alone in his pride in saying such things. Many people express this sentiment. Some of the "Not-Evers" are of Joe's generation, but the resistance to the use of digital media is not a product of age.

For many, reluctance to adopt new tools is motivated by a range of fears: elusive technical abilities ("I can't operate computers"), the potential to fail ("I might share something that will destroy my career"), or even a belief that technology will be a destructive force in our society ("The Internet is making us dumber."). Years spent developing a certain skillset and achieving a position of status could be undermined through misuse of digital media. The loss of control over branding messages seems implicitly detrimental.

Anthropologist Genevieve Bell, director of Intel Corporation's Interaction and Experience Research, has a theory that when a technology elicits negative reactions like these—especially the types of reaction that she calls "moral panic"—it is typically because the technology changed that person's relationship to time, to space, and other people [Bell, 2011]. Older technologies, like electricity, trains, and television, once triggered similar fears. Humans adapted.

The underlying assumption is that new technology deprecates everything we know, sending us into a debilitating cycle of re-learning. Indeed, some of the things we know, can do, or that help us frame the world are made *obsolete* by new technologies and situations. It is becoming less important, for example, to write down or memorize lists of phone numbers when they can easily be stored on a digital phone. The raw materials of today's success—knowledge, skill and mindset—are certainly different than those necessary two decades ago. However, not *all* things are completely new[1].

No new technology develops in a vacuum. Twitter rose in the wake of instant message status updates, mobile texting, and Internet Relay Chat (IRC). The same abilities acquired by use of these earlier systems provided a foundation for tweeting from a smartphone. The essentials of Twitter will undoubtedly become critical to mastering the next digital tool.

Take stock. Although perhaps not obvious initially, skills serving you well in the past may become the skills most useful for the digital age: typing prowess

[1]
There are five ways to alter what we know and can do: creation, retrieval, obsoletion, enhancement, and maintenance. These concepts are inspired by Marshall and Eric McLuhan's four laws of media [McLuhan, M. McLuhan, E. 1988]. Later in this chapter, we will apply this thinking to explain how you may or may not already be prepared to face change.

or understanding an argument, for example. Despite differences between former experiences and new technology, exisiting knowledge and skills will enhance the way digital technology is used.

Though the digital age looks different, past experiences are *maintained*, or even *enhanced*. If you are a great storyteller or good at telling truth from lies, you could find yourself using these abilities more often in digital communication than you did before.

Some elements of success may be missing from your experience. Innovation in technology often demands that we learn new knowledge, skills and mindset to help us make use of new systems. Understanding how viral memes spread, for example, is an ability *created* by new circumstances.

> There is a good chance you already have many of the things you will need to succeed in the digital age.

While many of these missing abilities will look new, some are actually *retrieved* from a previous era. The increasing need to use transparency to foster trust seems to be a byproduct of digital media, but it is a dormant phenomenon that was the norm prior to the Industrial Revolution[2]. From the 1500's through the 1700's, maritime business—absent a central control for communication between agents and ships—relied on a chain of mutually supporting partnerships to coordinate shipping and navigation. This kinship network, based on relational trust, was displaced during the rise of the corporation with more impersonal mechanisms of control and decision making.

Before we get further into our discussion of how the digital age adds and reconfigures abilities, it is worth a closer look at the three key components of *ability*.

2
The increasing use of communication technologies in the last 100 years has "..represented the beginning of a restoration— although with increasing centralization—of the economic and political control that was lost at more local levels of society during the Industrial Revolution." [Beniger, 1986]

Skills

Skills are the mental, verbal or physical manipulation of data or objects. The greater one's skill, the more able that person is to get desired results with minimal effort and maximal control. Skill impacts flexibility and creativity.

A lack of skill forms critical hurdles. Difficulty in typing, conducting Internet searches, or doing simple technical troubleshooting all create barriers to a person's desire to use digital technology. Advancing one's skills—editing photos, tagging content, or editing a wiki page—may be required to complete the journey to digital fluency.

Without appropriate skills to allow you to do what is needed, digital tools are unlikely to provide significant benefit to you or your organization.

Knowledge

At every stage of the learning process, people access factual or procedural information that will help (or hinder) their actions. Knowledge helps a person to make beneficial decisions[3].

3
The question of the nature of knowledge has a long history dating back hundreds, if not thousands of years. We offer this simple definition as a way of highlighting the distinction between knowing facts, being able to act, and the state of being which determines how facts are conceived and received by people.

Many people inhibit their own digital abilities with incorrect knowledge about the outcomes of social media use. Limited assertions blind people to potential and relevant value (e.g., "Twitter is only used to share what people had for lunch."). Incorrect knowledge might include a claim that there is one way to use social media. A step-by-step "do this not that" list may recognize desired outcomes, but it likely will constrain innovation or discount other benefits of using the system.

Mistakes are corrected through experience. Accurate knowledge of how social media is being used outside of the organization help to gain deep customer insights, discover breakthrough product innovations, improve productivity, or even coordinate disaster response. Knowledge should grow from more than a single source, such as a book or a seminar. It is honed by overcoming small failures through experimentation.

Mindset

Our point of view on the world—our mindset—colors everything we do, from the things we observe to the way we assign value to our abilities.

Decision makers with a technology-centric mindset might blame a choice of software for any difficulty employees experience using a digital collaboration platform. In response, they may purchase a new system, rather than investigate how people's skills, the company culture, or their own policies slowed the pace of adoption.

An organization with a strict message-control mindset might find it difficult to embrace a new mode of communication and learn from people outside the organization who post comments on the Internet about their brand (both negative and positive). Such an organization might adopt an adversarial and even aggressive response to those authors, rather than engage and nurture potential brand evangelists.

A balanced mindset feeds itself, inviting many new perspectives on digital technology and creating options for how those tools can help both an individual and the organization.

Ability	Description
Networking	The ability to search for, synthesize, and disseminate information.
Play	The capacity to experiment with one's surroundings as a form of creative problem-solving.
Performance	The ability to adopt alternative identities for the purpose of improvisation and discovery
Simulation	The ability to interpret and construct dynamic models for real-world processes
Appropriation	The ability to meaningfully sample and remix media content
Multitasking	The ability to scan one's environment and shift focus as needed to identify salient details
Distributed Cognition	The ability to interact meaningfully with tools that expand mental capacities
Collective Intelligence	The ability to pool knowledge and compare notes with others toward a common goal
Judgment	The ability to evaluate the reliability and credibility of different information sources
Transmedia Navigation	The ability to follow the flow of stories and information across multiple modalities
Negotiation	The ability to travel across diverse communities, discerning and respecting multiple perspectives, and grasping and following alternative norms
Visualization	The ability to interpret and create data representations for the purposes of expressing ideas, finding patterns, and identifying trends

Table 2.1
The twelve abilities relevant to the digital age, as drawn from
the work of Henry Jenkins.

Building Ability

A person's accumulated skills, knowledge and mindset together become the raw materials of developing ability which allow for flexibility, creativity and confidence in taking action. In the digital age, abilities can include searching with Google, or editing a Wikipedia article. These activities require some combination of knowledge (e.g., where the tools are located online) and skill (e.g., crafting effective search terms), as well as adopting a mindset that will allow action to begin and attempt to achieve a desired outcome.

An ability is the potential to take action in some specific way.

It may be helpful to group these into general types. There are a number of existing frameworks and models researchers and practioners have assembled to help clarify the concept of abilities. These include the iSkills assessment [ETS, 2002], New Literacies [Lankshear Knobel, 2006] and the New Media Literacies (NML) framework. We have found this last one, developed by Henry Jenkins [Jenkins, 2006], to be a helpful way to arrange the set of things a person needs to be able to act and succeed in the digital age (see Table 2.1).

It is not necessary here to detail the definitions and supporting evidence for Jenkin's list of ability types. However, later in Chapter 5, we use Jenkin's framework and the NML abilities as inspiration for twelve tasks you can do to start developing your digital fluency. For more information on NML, please explore the New Media Literacies Project website (http://newmedialiteracies. org/) hosted by USC Annenberg School of Communication and Journalism.

Prepared For Change

Maintaining abilities

Innovation isn't spontaneous. Rarely does it appear suddenly, accompanied by a radical paradigm shift. Twitter came about because texting and instant messaging already existed. Email was a faster and easier version of letter writing. Telephones were an improvement over the telegraph. Printing presses addressed limitations of hand reproduction New technology typically builds on established technology that came before it[4], leveraging the existing abilities of people using those systems.

Some of the knowledge, skills and mindsets needed to succeed are exactly the same as they were before the innovation.

What new technology requires of a fluent person is essentially the same as that demanded by earlier technologies. Communication involves people talking to other people and trying to exchange information to some effect. This is true whether the technology is a 1954 rotary dial landline, a 1994 mobile phone, or an online network facilitating VoIP. A fluent communicator should continue to flex that muscle regardless of the system.

Throughout our research, most of the people who showed an aptitude for using digital technology leveraged some pre-digital skill. Gifted storytellers still tell stories, but the potential forms of those stories now include a blog post, enabling the storyteller to engage her readers in asynchronous discussions from anywhere in the world. Those who love the sound of another person's voice

4
This process of new media technologies building on older technologies has been referred to as re-mediation [Bolter and Grusin, 2000].

are still having in-person conversations, but now those conversations continue online through voice and video chat. Musicians mix music using Garage Band, tinkerers share techniques through Make.com, makers sell their craft goods through Etsy.com, and photographers share and critique each other's photos on Flickr.com.

When new technology arrives, some of the knowledge, skills and mindset needed to succeed are the same as they were before the innovation.

Enhancing abilities

In his 1985 paper "Transforming of Western Style Management," iconic business researcher and thinker W. Edwards Deming laid out the 14 things he felt American management had to do to combat decline [Deming, 1985]. Point nine advised management to:

> *"Break down barriers between departments. People in research, design, sales, and production must work as a team, to foresee problems of production and in use that may be encountered with the product or service."*

Heeding Deming's 1985 admonition is even more important today. In the digital age, where problems are more complex, information naturally spreads across departments through the widespread individual use of social networks, blogs, and smartphones (often before official channels of communication can catch up). Whatever sense of teamwork and cooperation exists in an organization requires further refinement to prevent stagnation and eventually decline.

The way we talk is also affected. All conversations begin with ceremony, something to establish a social space[5].

5
In linguistics, this is referred to as a phatic message, a part of speech where the content isn't as important as the fact that something is being said. This may be informal ("Hi") or formal ("Good morning, may I please speak to Mrs. Thatcher?").

Before Bell Systems allowed direct dialing, human operators served this function, acting as an intermediary to two callers to make sure all parties were ready and willing to talk. By the time the parties began speaking to each other, the conversational space was already established.

Once technology existed to cut the operator out of the process, the responsibility for starting a conversation fell to the caller. Words chosen to initiate a dialogue now had direct impact on whether the person on the other end would be willing to stay on the line.

> Success evolves from what you are already doing, enhancing activities with which you are already engaged.

Similarly, by extending the possible context of a business call—from a worker sitting in an office with a land line to someone who could be anywhere—the mobile phone forced callers to be able to detect (or mask) the context of the call. No longer assuming that all background noise belonged to co-workers around a water cooler or working a copier, phone-fluent people listen for sounds of traffic, children, or nature to be able to better understand the situation in which the call was taking place. Callers know that the person at the other end may not be talking on a phone at all, but through a computer. Also, multiple digital channels (like Twitter) exist to help one understand the person's current situation, even before anyone begins dialling.

When new technology arrives, some existing knowledge, skills, and mindset need to be expanded to incorporate relevant information about the changing context. Success evolves from what you are already doing, enhancing activities with which you are already engaged.

Rethinking abilities

Dial phones brought a new sense of empowerment and privacy to Bell Systems customers, who no longer had to rely on an operator to facilitate (and perhaps listen to) their calls. That shift, though, also made some formerly useful skills irrelevant.

Operators were trained to rapidly switch wires to connect calling parties, and those who excelled often developed exceptional memories. Switchboards, or manual exchanges, were largely replaced with automated exchanges, lessening the need for these abilities. The effects on the need for memory became more widespread with the adoption of the modern cell phone.

There was a time when seven-digit numbers were etched into your brain. Long after friends moved away, phone numbers from years past remain easy to recite. Dialing someone today is less reliant on mental recall, or even manually keying in someone's number. Today, a computer in the phone keeps track, replacing digits with names. Our memory suffers from lack of practice.

Losing abilities can affect other qualities, like self-worth. The gregarious storytellers we previously mentioned were early adopters of voicemail technology. Prior to 2005, people frequently left each other encouraging messages and shared news through voicemail. They made good use of their excellent storytelling and conversational talents. As dependency on email grew, the frequency of such messages dropped dramatically and those skills atrophied—resulting in a sense of loss throughout the organization that the CEO described as a low level of grief.

With new technology, existing knowledge, skills and mindset may be hidden or even removed altogether as those abilities lose relevance.

Unprepared For Change

Creating new abilities

When Bell Systems transitioned from operator-assisted calls to manual dialing in 1954, they felt obligated to produce an instructional film to teach the public how to use their new phones. The introduction of a dial tone—which replaced a then-familiar "Number, please?"—was disconcerting to experienced customers, in much the same way its disappearance unsettled some cell phone users in the 1990s.

To be able to master the phone of the mid-1950s, even an experienced phone user had to gain new knowledge (e.g., understanding the meaning of a dial tone when picking up the receiver) and skills (e.g., moving the rotary dial around to correspond to the digits of a desired phone number).

New technology also requires some expanded notion of how the world works. Most people in 1994 knew of computers, but not necessarily the World Wide Web or even email. *Tron* (1982), *Wargames* (1983), S*neakers* (1992) and The Net (1995)were among only a handful of popular movies involving computing. Mostly, they focused on an underlying danger: Pierce Brosnan battling a computer genius, and Sandra Bullock being chased by digital identity thieves.

The Internet didn't provide widespread value to businesses, however, until people could see the potential benefit of 24/7 access to data and increased connections to people around the world, without regard to a shared place or time. To succeed in the digital age, a person must be able to appropriately weigh the practical risks and future benefits of new technology.

Retrieving old abilities

For many years, landline phones tethered people to time and space, forcing business conversations to take place only when both parties were sitting at their desks in an office. With cell phones, that connection is made outside of those constraints. For many people, the introduction of such technology afforded the rediscovery of mobility.

Mobility isn't something new to history, however. Humans arose from a tradition of hunters and gatherers, where following resources was a skillset critical to survival. While not life or death, many salespeople prefer to conduct phone conversations while traveling to client sites, rather than have to make those calls from behind a desk.

Trust is another beneficiary of digital media. The complexity and speed of interaction today allows people to quickly forward messages, videos and photos to their friends. This creates an environment where rumors spread rapidly. The speed of such misinformation was once mitigated by a slower pace of traditional media cycles and person-to-person contact. That information reached a person at all was reason enough for many to believe it.

Trust today extends to strangers and crowdsourced[6] content, placing a premium on ability to filter incoming information for relevance and validity. This increased need to foster trust with others harkens back to social dynamics that once played a large role in pre-industrial and tribal cultures[7].

When new technology arrives, some forgotten knowledge, skills and mindset resurface. By resurrecting critical abilities and restoring their value, you help yourself succeed in the new environment.

6
Crowdsourcing is a distributed problem-solving and production process that involves outsourcing tasks to a network of people, or crowd.

7
This general concept is well-documented [McLuhan, 1964; Pettit, 2007]. Sociologist James Beniger wrote that before the Industrial Revolution, government and markets depended on personal relationships and face-to-face interactions. In the late 1800's, that control shifted to the bureaucratic organization, a new infrastructure of transportations and telecommunications [Beniger, 1986].

Learning to adapt

In his 1971 book *Beyond the Stable State*, Donald Schön made the case that widespread use of technologies like computers and communication systems[8] were not only changed themselves, but they also became agents of change. The more we use tools that facilitate rapid innovation, the more the world forces us to innovate.

"[Facebook] humanizes people in a really nice way"

Shifts are inevitable. Complexity in the world—many diverse individuals making small decisions that affect others—guarantees that the circumstances today won't be quite the same tomorrow. Even minor changes have the potential to shake routines and question one's ability to function in the future. Highly adaptable people optimize their situation, taking their careers to unexpected places.

Ann, 50, is a director of a local retail store with a heavy focus on sustainable food. She considered digital technology antithetical to the spirit of her organization, but gradually, she began to use Facebook to correspond with co-workers and other people within her store's national organization. "Suddenly, there is this dimension of their lives that is visible to me that I hadn't expected to know about," she described. "I saw the full experience of life that people have in a way that is surprisingly intimate, but at a proximity that is still respectful. It humanizes people in a really nice way."

8
Schön wrote this well before widespread public use of the World Wide Web, the appearance of which would have supported his claims even further.

Adaptation is what allows us to use our abilities effectively when shifting between contexts, usually in response to the changing world around us. It draws from knowledge and relevant skills from prior experience, and allows us to see change as an opportunity to learn. Adaptation is critical to the ongoing learning required for digital fluency (the topic of the next chapter) .

> Dropped my laptop on floor this morning. I usually drop my phone, so good to know I'm moving on to bigger and better things.

12:28 PM May 28th, 2009 via txt

zappos
Zappos.com CEO - Tony

Zappos

Zappos.com is a highly successful customer service company that happens to sell goods. Though many people view the company's highly innovative methods as original, they are in fact quite familiar, albeit transformed. Their transparent use of digital media, for example, requires skills that people developed in pre-industrial days when the line between the inside and the outside of an organization wasn't quite as distinct. People knew the owner of the general store not through the PR department, but by looking over the counter.

The five largest Twitter accounts of Zappos employees have a social media audience of around 1.75 million followers [Zappos, 2010], which makes them a large part of the company's marketing efforts. These employees, however, hold the titles of CEO, Director of Operations, Chief Operating Officer, and Community Architect, none of which includes the word "marketing."

At one point, CEO Tony Hsieh posted an average of 4.3 Twitter messages a day to his 800,000 followers. The text of these messages blurred the boundary between organizational and everyday roles by alternating between serious business matters (e.g., Hsieh openly discussed his company's acquisition by Amazon.com on July 22, 2009) and quirky personal news or observations (see above). This same medium allows Hsieh to be warmly perceived as both corporate and human, reinforcing the culture of Zappos.

"Electric writing and speed pour upon him, instantaneously and continuously, the concerns of all other men. He becomes tribal once more."

—MARSHALL MCLUHAN

A Box of Future

A single package is on her desk when Louise arrives at the office. From the shape and size, she can guess what is inside, but she isn't ready for that future. With a quick turn on her heel, Louise procrastinates by getting a cup of coffee.

As she pours the dark brew into a mug, Louise remembers when her thinking began to shift. On a rainy night in the city, a young man offered to share a taxi to keep them both from getting drenched. Chit-chat revealed him to be an engineer at a small auto parts manufacturer, and a father of four. They didn't speak much during that drive, but Louise saw the tablet device in his lap. As she sips her coffee now, Louise replays their conversation in her head .

"I'm sort of glad they can reach me, if there's a problem," the man had said, noticing her interest. "But I also sort of wish they couldn't, too."

Offering her a better glance at the screen, Louise studied a video of a foreman pointing to a smoking machine. She recalls recognizing the mechanical problem at fault, having seen it many times before. Her rolled-up *Boston Globe* pointed at the screen. "Looks to me like the A2 coolant hose. Have you checked it?" Cocking his head, the man paused. He typed a message using keys that appeared on the screen. A second later, he had smiled: "No, apparently we haven't."

Two weeks ago, Louise sat in a meeting with her leadership team. She didn't lead the discussion about a technology upgrade, but she had been able to understand the suggestion that tablets might be a good fit for Superior Machinery. She remembers leaning forward on her chair when talk turned to how the devices would allow managers to stay informed while moving from team to team. Today, a box waits on her desk, the outcome of that meeting.

Louise remains anxious about the technology she is about to touch for the first time. She knows and perhaps agrees with the arguments for why it arrived, but Louise has doubts. How much will the device interfere with her routines? How long will it take to learn how to use it? She won't have to find out until she opens the package.

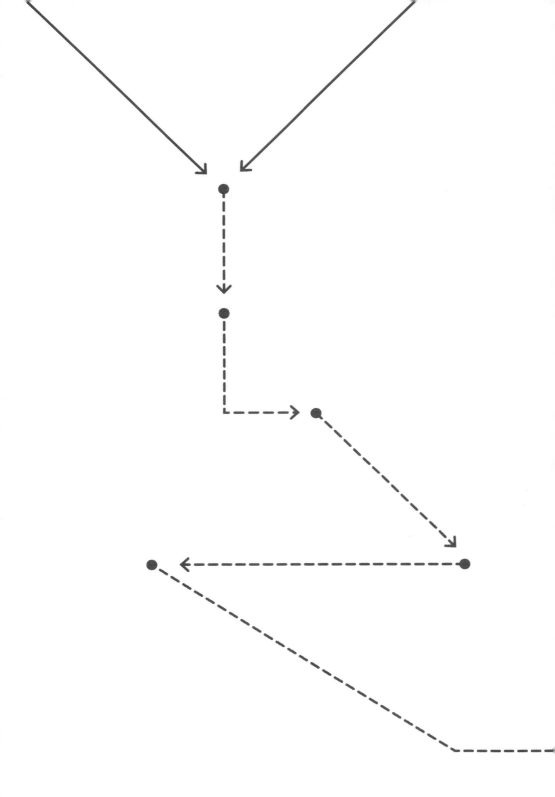

3

Becoming Fluent

The development and maintenance of digital fluency is an ongoing process

A minor composer in Salzburg during the 18th century proved to be a better teacher than a performer. He wrote a tutorial in 1755 that established his reputation in the music community. Just as his career was taking off, the composer had a son, his second child.

On a lark, the father began teaching his kids to play the clavier (keyboard). During sessions with his 7-year-old daughter, his 3-year-old boy looked on. It wasn't long before the boy started picking out chords that sounded appealing to him. After a while, his father took notice and gave him formal instruction on a few minuets, which he played flawlessly and in perfect time.

By age 5, Wolfgang Amadeus Mozart was composing and performing his own pieces. At the time of his death only 30 years later, Mozart had originated more than 600 works, including some of the most lasting and influential music in history. Today, most people will agree that music came naturally to Mozart.

For most of us, fluency is not achieved this easily. Few people are able to start tapping on keys one day and be considered a prodigy the next. Developing fluency takes both time and maintenance.

This is particularly true of digital abilities. Email is a well-established digital channel, for example, but its use causes new problems as life gets faster and more connected. Skills such as typing and writing a persuasive argument remain useful. As newer technology like Facebook displaces email as a dominant means of communication, new skills are required. Fluency now involves a willingness to craft semi-public messages and managing complicated and ever-changing privacy settings.

Many people with the ability to use one form of technology quite well struggle to apply those relevant skills to newer tools. While researching this book, we met:

- close-knit teams of tech-savvy storytellers who dreaded company social networks

- experienced public relations professionals who were duped by false information

- IT professionals and programmers who did not want or know how to use online collaboration platforms

- talkative, insightful, wordsmiths unable to work within the constraints of Twitter's 140 characters

- people experienced with radical social innovation who hesitated to engage their customers online, for fear of making mistakes.

In every case, failure was not caused by an overall lack of ability. Rather, changes surrounding these people altered the available tools and technology. The context shifted, leaving them without the knowledge, skills, and mindset necessary to take action.

Experience Is Critical

First-hand experience is the best way to develop the knowledge, skills, and mindset that leads to fluency. Some knowledge can be gained by reading books like this one, of course, but deeper understanding can only be developed through regular use.

This cannot be overemphasized: As with language fluency, or fluency with a musical instrument, the development and maintenance of digital abilities *requires practice*. Because first-hand experience is so critical to learning, the process to become fluent demands an investment of time and patience, with ourselves and with those around us.

> First-hand experience is the best way to develop the abilities that lead to fluency.

In early March 2009, Mars candy brand Skittles replaced the home page of their website with a raw stream of Twitter status updates[1]. On the surface, the choice was a bold endorsement of the value of social media. No initial effort was made, however, to filter or engage with the content that consumers were providing. This allowed the site to become a gamed environment for crude and even racist content, posted in the name of the company. Those early mistakes allowed the agency to reflect on their experiences, modify assumptions, and evolve the Skittles site into a positive case study for digital media integration.

The pace of learning is different for everyone. For some, a first blog post is a simple matter of sitting down and typing. For others, it may take years to gain comfort in sharing personal thoughts online. Experimentation through first-hand experience can help dramatically speed up this learning process.

[1] The social media strategy concocted by Agency.com also included similar experiments with Wikipedia and Facebook. Learning from early mistakes, Skittles eventually created an "unsite" that directly leveraged various social media platforms. Less than a year after the experiment started, Skittles' Facebook page had over 3.6 million fans, and their reach had multiplied 2-3 times what it once was [Assi, 2010].

Digital Fluency

Most of us have an idea of what it means to be fluent. People who are fluent in speaking French are able to go to Paris and converse with residents on subjects of mutual interest. A fluent reader is somebody who understands what she is reading quickly and with minimum effort. In general, most people know fluency as a level of skill that makes something look natural when you do it.

> **Fluency is the ability to reliably achieve desired outcomes through the use of technology.**

There is something else, though: implicit in fluency is a goal. A fluent reader knows grammar, can read, and believes the printed word is an efficient and entertaining way to consume information, all of which enables her to get some enjoyment out of finishing a text. A person fluent in French knows the vocabulary, has mastered French pronunciation, and can appropriate a Frenchman's world view, all of which allows him to have a heated debate about international politics with a shopkeeper on rue Cler. There is both a motivation to use and an outcome for fluency, not just a possibility.

This is a critical distinction to make when it comes to leveraging fluency within an organization. Successful organizations act with purpose toward an envisioned goal. For our purposes, we offer the following definition:

> *Fluency is an ability to reliably achieve desired outcomes through use of technology.*

Let us illustrate this take on fluency with a true story, relayed to us by a local business man.

A few years ago, Tom (the business man) took a trip to Mexico to import a large shipment of wine for his business. At the border, a customs official caused some trouble for Tom and his brother, who was helping with the shipment. Although Tom spoke little Spanish, his brother had lived in the country for many years. After a few rounds of negotiations with the elderly customs official, Tom's brother returned and in angry whispers, let loose a flurry of comments about the stubbornness of the man. Desperate to move through the red tape, Tom suggested that *he* might be able to sway the official.

Leaving his brother somewhat amused, Tom walked to the official. Smiling warmly, he cobbled together words he knew well with ones he just heard his brother say, in reference to the official, and greeted the customs officer: "Qué pasa, Señor Pelón." After a moment, the official and his fellow agents burst out laughing. What Tom did not realize was that *pelón*—the Spanish word for bald—was not the man's name, but just a slur blurted out by Tom's brother in anger. Whether his gaffe hurt the negotiation isn't known, but it certainly was not what Tom expected.

By our definition, Tom was not fluent in Spanish because he lacked the ability needed to produce his desired outcome. Tom overestimated his understanding of the language. He did not recognize the nuance of his brother's disdain muttered in Spanish and failed to use the right words to get his meaning across. Instead of approaching a frustrated customs official with respect, he had insulted the man.

In order to fully understand what fluency is, we must also explore what it is not. For this reason, we need to introduce a second term, *literacy*, defined as a less-advanced version of fluency. A literate person would understand what to do and how to do it, but would not be able to articulate the when and why.

When Tom the businessman spoke Spanish, he knew enough about the grammar and pronunciation for his words to be understood. He could also hear someone else speak and recognize it as Spanish enough to pull a greeting out of the context. Tom was (barely) literate in Spanish because he understood, at a minimal level, how to speak and what to say.

However, Tom was not fluent. He failed to understand that *pelón* in that context was a description, not a name. He didn't know, either, why the customs officials broke into laughter as he greeted them in what he thought was a respectful manner. Even if he had used the official's name correctly, Tom lacked any comprehension of when it might be appropriate to use the informal "Qué pasa?" ("What's up?") and why it is a sign of disrespect in Mexican culture.

The relationship between abilities and desired outcomes applies to any technology, including digital. A digitally literate person may know what Twitter is and how to tweet, but he wouldn't understand why posting a link to a web article that strays from his expertise could prove valuable, or when posting that information would have the greatest impact. For a person to achieve her goals, he needs to have moved beyond just the what and how to an understanding of the when and the why[2].

We live in a time when digital materials and tools are pervasive; most societies cannot function without touching digital technology in some way. For that reason, our definition becomes more specific:

> ***Digital fluency*** *is an ability to reliably achieve desired outcomes* ***through use of digital technology***.

A person who consistently develops and maintains their abilities with digital tools will be more likely to achieve

[2] Others have described new literacies as the ability to use the "technical stuff" and the "ethos stuff" of a technology [Lankshear and Knobel, 2006].

what they expect than someone who is content with literacy alone.

Digital fluency does not guarantee a desired outcome, however. Factors outside of an individual's control—such as work environment, or market volatility—also impact success. This requires an addendum to our previous definition:

> Digital fluency is an ability to reliably achieve desired outcomes through use of digital technology. **This ability is helped or hindered by the situational forces and the digital fluency of others.**

From our non-digital example, if Tom the businessman were fluent enough in Spanish to avoid the problems he encountered, his fluency alone might not be sufficient to get his imported wine past customs. The context surrounding his conversation might make it impossible to succeed. A fluent Tom may have still failed if:

- the government issued temporary orders to prevent all goods from leaving the country

- the customs official had fought with his wife earlier that morning and was having a bad day

- his brother argued the wrong point

- one of the officials misread a label on the wine.

Fluency gives a person the *best possible chance* of succeeding, given what is within his control.

These complicating factors influence an organization's *digital readiness*[3], or its ability to create an optimal situation to support individual digital fluency. Throughout this book, we focus on how an individual

[3] This is the focus of our second book.

creates a "best scenario for success" and will, for now, de-emphasize the organizational context . The reality, however, is that the rest of the world always has something to say about success.

Obviously, not all fluencies are the same. The differences between speaking a foreign language, critiquing a book, and engaging customers through digital media arise from both the properties of the technology being used and the context of that use. Tom's business savvy doesn't make him fluent in Spanish, any more than his struggles in communicating with the Mexican customs official mean he can't communicate effectively on Twitter or Facebook.

What makes digital fluency particularly challenging is *how* it is qualitatively different from earlier forms of fluency.

In our earlier telephone example, fluency was maintained by responding to changes largely contained within a single industry and technology. With digital technology, the sheer number of systems one must experience to become fluent may seem daunting. Each digital tool has its own way of providing value. People often employ multiple tools and strategies at the same time, making it necessary to acknowledge that there is no one way to "do it right" if a person is to achieve fluency.

Older tools are not always replaced with digital ones. Even as Voice over IP (VoIP), automatic message transcriptions, and the market penetration of mobile devices altered when and why a phone call is useful, the telephone is still in use. Digital fluency is in many ways more difficult to build and to maintain because of the speed and complexity that digital technologies have introduced into the world (see Figure 1.1 in Chapter 1).

Four Stages of Learning

Imagine yourself back in 1994 as an Early Adopter, someone who tries technology before it reaches critical mass. The World Wide Web was too new to be of critical use to your business, but the mobile phone had become your main means of conducting business. Texting was possible, but rarely used (you never did). By making calls on the road, you learned the importance of recharging. You became skilled at managing usage minutes to minimize cost and maximize information exchanged during a call.

By our definition, we could say that in 1994, you were mobile phone fluent.

> To remain fluent in 2012, you need more ability than what made you savvy in 1994.

Jump ahead to 2012. The phone may still be an important part of your business process—clients and co-workers know they can reach you at any time—but much about the digital landscape has changed. Texting is common, so much so that new laws are in place to prevent use of the phone while driving. Phones became "smart," as well as mobile. They understand where you are and can connect to the Internet to send and retrieve information. Cell phones might not be good for writing reports or programming, but they are loaded with applications for checking email and interacting with your network, as if you were at your computer. Technology has evolved, blurring the line between work and personal time.

To remain mobile phone fluent in 2012, you need more abilities than what made you savvy in 1994. Without any adjustment, you might still see your communication options as calling, writing a letter, or making an appointment—all during traditional business hours—and miss ways to communicate instantly and asynchronously[4] via email or Facebook. You might miss seeing the web as a useful way to broadcast information 24 hours a day, let alone automate some conversations with clients. Fluency is never a static achievement. Without new experiences, the same tools will become less useful over time.

> Fluency is never a static achievement. Without new experiences, the same abilities become less useful over time.

This dynamic journey to fluency is a process built on change, comprised of four stages: *Anti-Literate*, *Pre-Literate*, *Literate*, and *Fluent*[5]. Each transition brings a little more knowledge, a few more skills, and a different way of looking at the world, allowing your abilities to improve and adapt.

4
Asynchronous communication happens when an exchange between people does not occur at the same time, such as a blog or web forum. A telephone conversation is not asynchronous.

5
This process is a simplified combination of the Dreyfus model of skill acquisition [Dreyfus and Dreyfus, 1980, 1986] and the Four Stages of Competence model.

Anti-Literacy

Far more people in this world do *not* use Twitter than do. There are many valid reasons to reject the microblogging service. An Anti-Literate person, however, rejects the possibility that there would be *any* value in Twitter, coming to that conclusion without having experienced the service enough to understand its affordances and limitations. The defining characteristic of an Anti-Literate person is not a lack of knowledge, but the refusal to acquire new knowledge (see Table 3.1, on next page).

> The defining characteristic of an Anti-Literate person is a refusal to acquire new knowledge.

In some ways, the Anti-Literate stage of the learning process may be the most difficult to move beyond. Much about digital media—its uses, potential value, operations, and effects—is still quite foreign to an Anti-Literate person. That makes it easy to resist. What keeps one Anti-Literate is an incomplete or neglected collection of raw materials to use in developing abilities. Either a few key bits of knowledge or skills are missing, or a dominating mindset on familiar abilities needs to be discarded.

An Anti-Literate person resists being drawn into the next stage of learning for a variety of reasons. A few common motivations include:

> *Being left behind*—When friends and family are doing things you don't understand, that feeling can spark a desire to be better informed. Grandparents often cite their kids' and grandkids' use of digital media as the reason they started using a computer.

Knowledge	Assumes that technology, not people, always dictates success
	Assumes that increased Internet use always decreases face-to-face communication
Skills	Has trouble typing, searching, or using a mouse
	Has difficulty troubleshooting basic computer problems
Mindset	Believes that playful things cannot be used for serious purposes
	Believes that technology is inherently good or evil

Table 3.1
Signs of digital
anti-literacy

Realizing play is serious business—Ten million people play the game World of Warcraft, improving real-world communication and leadership skills through its social mechanisms. Twitter is often perceived a soapbox for the trivial and mundane[6], but the low barrier to sharing such information (and things of more substance, too) proves an effective means of building valuable collaboration networks. At some point, a suspicion surfaces that digital services are more useful and serious than they appear.

Seeing possibility—Competition can change one's mind about a particular technology. It is easier to see potential value in digital media when peers experience success by using it[7].

When revelations like these occur in an Anti-Literate individual, it is a strong indication that Pre-Literacy is achievable.

6
See Chapter 1,
pp. 24-25 for an
example of how
the mundane can
translate into fiscal
savings.

7
There is a long
tradition of
psychological
research on these
sorts of phenomena
that is called social
learning theory,
pioneered by Albert
Bandura. [Bandura,
1977]

Pre-Literacy

In the face of new technology, a Pre-Literate person recognizes something is gained by addressing one's lack of ability. Whereas the Anti-Literate rejected the idea that a tool like Twitter provides any value, a Pre-Literate person will be open to discovering its potential, improving his knowledge, skills and mindset to do so (see Table 3.2, on next page).

This stage is characterized by extensive knowledge gaps.

A Pre-Literate person recognizes something is gained by addressing one's lack of ability.

With Twitter, the low-hanging fruit consists of knowing what a tweet is, what it means to put a pound sign (#) in front of a word[8], and whether posted content can be permanently deleted. New skills—many unknown to a Pre-Literate—are needed to follow people and effectively manage a social network.

Perhaps most importantly, the ways in which Pre-Literate people approach digital tools are not fully developed. Being comfortable with sharing personal information in public spaces—despite the loss of control such message distribution entails—is a critical mindset for successfully using digital media. It is equally important to understand that Twitter is not a magic-bullet solution for all challenges an organization may face.

Motivation to overcome shortcomings in knowledge, skills and mindset helps advance the individual to the Literate stage in the learning process. This includes:

Finding heroes—Once a person can imagine value in using digital technology, awareness of digital

[8]
Hashtags are words or phrases prefixed with the pound symbol (#). They are used in Twitter and other social platforms as a meta tag to group content by topic.

Knowledge	Does not know technical terms
	Understands the potential value of using a technology
Skills	Has difficulty using basic tools of digital technology
	Is able to imagine one's self in a future state
Mindset	Oversimplifies or underestimates the role of new technology
	Believes change is necessary

Table 3.2
Signs of digital
pre-literacy

role models—people who are perceived as more active and knowledgeable about the tools—leads to a desire to emulate their actions. Developing literacy arises from a desire to use the digital technology in the same way as someone who uses it successfully.

Finding the silver bullet—When Fluent users make using the tools appear easy, Pre-Literate people may be inspired to take the next step, perceiving digital media to be a quick and simple solution to big problems. While this perception is beneficial to advance one's learning, it may lead to overestimation of the power of the tools or an underestimation of the time involved, making using these tools look easy.

Literacy

Literate people have acquired basic abilities that allow for the full use of digital technology (see Table 3.3, on next page). They know, for example, what a tweet is and how to associate it with a topic using a hashtag. They can conduct a simple search for brands and trending topics, and they might recognize a popular meme[9]. There is a perceived value in using digital tools, even if their appreciation is limited to a single kind of use (e.g., only posting web links). Being Literate means knowing what to do and how to do it.

> **Being Literate means knowing what to do and how to do it.**

For many, this stage of the learning process seems like the end of the journey. With more frequent use of digital media, however, the Literate person begins to notice a few new challenges.

While it worked well initially, a 5-step "best practices" checklist for using Twitter will backfire. A status update posted as a joke to 100 followers might receive angry replies from a few dozen readers. Managing the onslaught of information feels like a full-time job, cutting into otherwise productive time. Knowing what to do and how to do it is no longer enough.

Moving beyond the Literate stage is a transition that can be triggered in a number of ways, most notably:

> *Experiencing breakdown*—Despite a basic understanding of how a tool works, frequent use of digital technology often brings unexpected results. This disconnect between what a person expects to happen and the actual outcome can reveal crucial abilities missing from the toolbox[10].

9
Richard Dawkins coined the term "meme," referring to a unit of cultural transmission or imitation like "tunes, ideas, catch-phrases, clothes fashions that propagate themselves in the meme pool by leaping from brain to brain via a process which, in the broad sense, can be called imitation" [Dawkins, 1976].

10
The idea is a long tradition in the philosophical writings of folks like Heidegger, Leont'ev, and Dewey [Koschmann, et al., 1998] who claim that an important way people learn is when normal functions break down.

Knowledge	Cites the number of posts, tweets, or followers as a key metric for success
	Understands different kinds of value from using digital media
Skills	Uses digital technology in prescribed ways, often missing errors in etiquette
	Copies the methods other people use for digital media
Mindset	Feels the tools have been mastered, or that there is one "right way" to use digital technologies

Table 3.3
Signs of digital
literacy

Making the tool work differently—At some point, most people realize that technology designed for one use can be appropriated in other ways to achieve a goal. Jack Dorsey imagined urban and office awareness when he created Twitter, not an earthquake warning system[11]. With this realization, a Literate person begins to imagine and experiment, discovering other ways digital media can support their goals.

These motivations are part of the complex mix that may move a person into the Fluent stage of learning.

11
Fourteen-year-old Sebastian Alegria from Chile appropriated Twitter to develop a $75 earthquake warning system, @AlarmaSismos, that warns tens of thousands of people 5 to 30 seconds before earthquakes hit.

Fluency

As abilities move beyond the what and how of digital media use, a Fluent person also understands *why* the use is important and *when* it is appropriate, or inappropriate. Except when reflecting on your past experiences, there is no need to think deeply about your use of the tool. Decisions become second-nature, or "easy." As the world around us continues to change, fluent people adapt (see Table 3.4, on next page).

> **Being Fluent means knowing when to do something and why you do it.**

Though not immune to mistakes, it is rare that a Fluent person commits a serious social gaffe. When mistakes do occur, the error is addressed in an authentic and often public manner, to turn the experience into a positive interaction with others.

In 2011, Gloria Huang accidentally posted a personal tweet—*"Ryan found two more 4 bottle packs of Dogfish Head's Midas Touch beer...when we drink we do it right #gettngslizzerd."*—to the official Red Cross Twitter account, read by 270,000 followers. The organization acknowledged the mistake quickly with a humorous post, earning goodwill for their honesty. Dogfish, the beer company mentioned in the tweet, responded by organizing a blood drive under the hashtag *#gettngslizzerd*[12].

A common misconception is that a person's use of digital technology increases with their level of fluency. Many assume that the person who uses her mobile device in the middle of meetings, or who camps out on sidewalks overnight to buy the newest technology, is the most fluent. Being digitally fluent does not equate with being techie.

12
Dogfish Head Brewery encouraged pubs and breweries distributing their product to encourage beer fans to donate a pint of blood to Red Cross and get a free pint as a reward [Segall, 2011]

Knowledge	Knows examples where digital technology is being used in ways that were not intended
	Envisions potential new uses for digital technology
Skills	Adapts to changing norms within a sub-community of users on a digital platform
	Jumps from one kind of digital technology to another to advance a goal
Mindset	Is comfortable with the fact that there is no "best" way to use a technology across all contexts
	Embraces change as opportunity

Table 3.4
Signs of digital
fluency

In fact, a Fluent person may use these tools *less* often, aligning activities with larger goals and discerning which circumstances would be helpful or detrimental to those goals. Making a phone call, or scheduling a face-to-face meeting may prove a better choice than communicating with a public post to Twitter. Fluency is as much about the *why not* as the why.

Two stages of learning (Anti-Literacy and Literacy) are particularly ripe for stagnation because the need for change is not readily apparent.

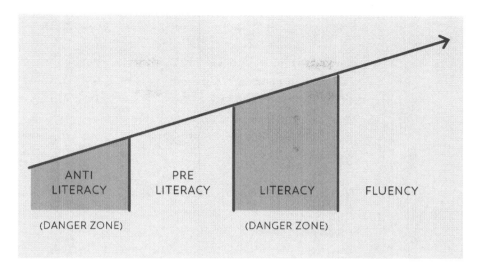

The Dangers Within

Figure 3.1.
The four stages
of digital
fluency

Because the development and maintenance of digital fluency is an ongoing activity, finding the motivation to continue to grow is critical. Along the journey, there are risks of complacency, danger zones where what you know or what you can do is deemed sufficient, causing the process to stall (see Figure 3.1).

In the Anti-Literate stage, the biggest challenge a person faces is seeing *any* value in the use of digital media. If that person waits too long to broaden mindset to allow for exploration, the rejected knowledge and skills may end up becoming an integral part of day-to-day business. Key pieces of information may be missed, causing susceptibility to scams or other forms of manipulation. A lack of mainstream skills could threaten job performance.

Similarly, a Literate person may not see value in continuing on with the learning process. Knowing enough to make use of digital technologies without the experience to achieve desired outcomes may create a false sense of accomplishment.

Some examples of use that could produce unwanted results include unintentionally leaking proprietary company information, surfing the Internet during important meetings, or starting a flame war (i.e., an online fight). Literate people are sometimes just knowledgeable enough to draw incomplete conclusions about the value of digital technology, prompting them to abandon further exploration.

These two stages—Anti-Literacy and Literacy—are particularly ripe for stagnation because the need for change is not readily apparent. The defining characteristic of Pre-Literacy is the recognition that change is required. The most important benefit of achieving Fluency is the ability to adapt to constant change. Anti-Literate people don't see a need to change, and Literate people view change as already overcome.

Digital fluency doesn't occur all at once. It evolves through the four stages, adapting knowledge, skills and mindset to the demands of a changing world. This is helped along with first-hand experiences. While each stage in this journey presents its own unique challenge, the Anti-Literate and Literate stages hold the greatest danger for stagnation, where people are content to stop learning.

Building and maintaining digital fluency are part of the ongoing learning process that will likely need to accelerate in the coming years. The effects of digital fluency must always happen in context, often impacted by external forces. In the next chapter, we will explore the role that your organization plays in your ability to succeed.

Rewind

What we've covered so far

Stage	Knowledge	Skills	Mindset
Anti-Literate	Assumes that technology, not people, always dictates success Assumes that increased Internet use always decreases face-to-face communication	Has trouble typing, searching, or using a mouse Has difficulty troubleshooting basic computer problems	Feels that playful things cannot be used for serious purposes Feels that technology is inherently good or evil
Pre-Literate	Does not know technical terms Understands the potential value of using a technology	Has difficulty using basic tools of digital technology Is able to imagine one's self in a future state	Oversimplifies or underestimates the role of new technology Believes change is necessary
Literate	Cites the number of posts, tweets, or followers as a key metric for success Understands different kinds of value from using digital media	Uses digital technology in prescribed ways, often missing errors in etiquette Copies the methods other people use for digital media	Feels the tools have been mastered, or that there is one "right way" to use digital technologies
Fluent	Knows examples where digital technology is being used in ways that were not intended Envisions potential new uses for digital technology	Adapts to changing norms within a sub-community of users on a digital platform Jumps from one kind of digital technology to another to advance a goal	Is comfortable with the fact that there is no "best" way to use a technology across all contexts Embraces change as opportunity

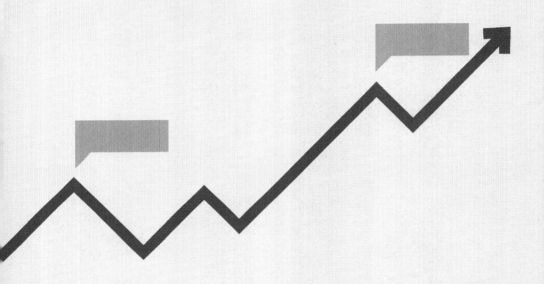

"[P]eople are more creative and productive when they are deeply engaged in the work, when they feel happy, and when they think highly of their projects, coworkers, managers and organizations."

—TERESA AMABILE

Sharing Happiness

Louise doesn't like the big screen mounted on the opposite wall outside her office. It cost a lot and seems like a distraction from the smaller screens on her employees' desks. Louise herself glances up from her own work several times a day to stare at it. No, she doesn't like the screen, but she is intrigued by what is on it.

Recently, one of her salespeople brought in an IT staffer to pitch Louise on the idea of showing information about the company on a large monitor, visible to everyone in the office. Featured would be a rotation of headlines about business clients, pictures of employees working in the community, and status updates about current projects. The kicker, Louise recalls, was that he wanted anyone in the organization to be able to control what appears on that screen.

As Louise assembled an advisory group to explore alternative ways to evaluate the investment, her CFO resisted. Like herself, he held concerns about buying equipment the company didn't need and setting up employees to be less productive ("They'll watch TV all day."). Even now, Louise fights those same fears and continues to trust her advisors.

Taking her eyes off of the big screen, Louise looks around the office and sees something new—smiles. It isn't as if her employees hated coming to work before, but there is a different hum to the workday. More people are eating lunch together and talking about their kids. They are also collaborating across departments, connections that didn't exist a year ago. She doesn't know if it is related to that monitor, but Superior Machinery is a happier place.

The phone on her desk rings. She answers, discovering her most troublesome client on the other end of the line. As she always does, Louise pulls a manila folder from her desk drawer, the portfolio for that account. However, it remains closed on her desk. Instead, Louise talks about a recent article she saw earlier that day on the big screen. It mentions an award the client just won. A few sentences into the phone conversation, Louise smiles, too.

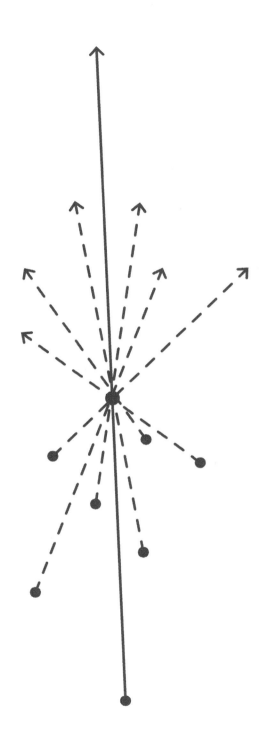

DIGITAL FLUENCY

4

Success In Context

Organizations play a big role in turning individual digital fluency into success

Even the most digitally fluent person cannot succeed unless the surrounding forces are set up to help her out. Success is a team game. It requires both the cooperation of others who are fluent and policies and resources of a supportive organization. We refer to the quality of this supporting context as *digital readiness*.

Digital readiness arises from a complex combination of factors which include:

- the roles people play in the organization
- the things that they are allowed to do
- the information available to them
- the costs and benefits associated with their actions
- the rules or norms which affect all of these things

When these factors are combined effectively, those in the organization with digital fluency are valued and rewarded by the emergence of real goals within a shared vision. The skill of one person won't determine success, however; it requires use of the whole buffalo[1]. To create a culture of success, it is essention to measure results in many ways and report findings to the rest of the organization.

[1] An old philosophy attributed to American Indians of the Plains urged hunters to use every part of each buffalo they killed. This saying has become a touchstone for sustainability and finding creative value in all of the materials a resource contains.

Digital Readiness

The interwoven forces that work together to support a successful organization are revealed in the research of political economist Elinor Ostrom[2]. She and her colleagues at Indiana University spent decades studying complex institutions dealing with collective action situations all over the world [Ostrom, 2011].

Ostrom's institutional analysis and development (IAD) framework is a key part of ongoing research at SociaLens, exploring the interdependent dynamics of organizations trying to operate in the digital age. For the purposes of this book, we take a closer look at an important subset of the IAD framework. Included are the things an organization can do to help cultivate success: providing tools and resources, promoting and supporting an evolving organizational culture, clarifying purpose, and seeking alignment between all of these activities.

Providing Tools and Resources

Seymour Papert, a pioneer in artificial intelligence, wrote of people who held extreme views of technology that they felt that either computers alone would solve all of our problems[3], or that digital technology would dehumanize us and disrupt the workplace and the economy.

Papert claimed such people focused on the wrong end of the techno-human relationship [Papert, 1987]:

The question is not 'What will the computer do to us?'
The question is 'What will we make of the computer?'
The point is not to predict the computer future. The point is to make it .

When an organization implements new software or hardware, the decision-makers must be aware of the unique set of benefits and constraints each tool brings to bear on the goals of the organization. In addition, this value must be clearly communicated to those using the new tools. Poor results are not necessarily a result of the qualities of the chosen technology, but rather the mismatch between the new technology and the other resources (including human) provided by the organization to support its use.

> Acquisition of technology alone is not sufficient to guarantee a benefit from use.

The purchase of a new customer management software platform (a financial investment) may provide powerful new capabilities to the employees who use it. However, installing that software also demands an investment of additional resources—time to train employees, strategic planning, political backing, and IT support—to facilitate the software's adoption. Acquisition of the technology alone is not sufficient to guarantee a benefit from its use.

Evolving Organizational Culture

The relationship between digital media and organizational culture has a relationship similar to the one in an old Bill Cosby joke about cocaine[4]—what you are is enhanced, not invented by technology. Because digital tools help people express ideas and disseminate information, more input exists to shape an online identity. The flaws of an organization are amplified along with its strengths.

4
Comedian Bill Cosby used to tell a joke where he asked someone to explain what it is about cocaine that makes it appealing to the people who use it: "The guy said, 'Well, it intensifies your personality.' I said, 'What if you're an a**hole?" [Cosby, 1983].

If the gestalt of a company is Pre-Literate—an uninformed acceptance of potential benefit of new technology— introducing new digital technology may simply reinforce those attitudes. Suspicious people may be more leery, focusing their anxiety toward new tools, raising resistance. Political or emotional divides between departments become more pronounced, particularly if the groups exhibit different degrees of digital fluency.

Digital readiness includes both a clear purpose and the ability to effectively navigate toward that end.

When the benefits of digital media are not understood, an organizational culture will likely experience failure trying to add it to existing routines. In fact, it is possible greater damage is done by requiring such tools before the organization is ready to succeed.

On the other hand, if the organization's culture fosters trust between colleagues and values learning, using digital media will most likely surface these traits. Its use will breed internal solidarity and comfort with sharing one's humanity with others (e.g., transparency).

Fluency with digital tools creates a virtuous cycle. The digital readiness of the organization is likely to improve if the organization has already evolved their culture to exhibit fluent traits, such as experimentation and the ability to rapidly switch contexts.

Netflix

The distinction between setting a vision and acting on it is illustrated by Netflix's 2011 pricing changes.

To the dismay of their customers, Netflix executives decided that streaming video would provide a better future than renting physical DVDs via mail, the company's signature service. Having weathered initial customer reaction to that first change, co-founder and CEO Reed Hastings announced another adjustment. In a rambling explanation—a blog post that drew more than 25,000 comments in two days—Hastings declared that Netflix would split their DVD business into a separate company, Qwikster.

Netflix gained potential strategic value in making these moves. The execution, however, was sloppy. One indication of the organization's lack of digital readiness was the decision to brand the company before investigating how that name was being used online (see Figure 4.1). Jason Castillo, owner of the Qwikster Twitter account, quickly attempted to capitalize on his good fortune with a six-figure payday—which the company didn't pay. One month after making the announcement, Netflix killed plans for Qwikster

No matter how Netflix resolved their social media identity, this lack of awareness reflected poorly on the company.

Figure 4.1
Jason Castillo's @qwikster Twitter account, created a few months prior to the announcement, gained more than 10,000 new followers in two days when a savvy customer base sought information about the new Netflix company. Instead, they found a pot-smoking Elmo avatar tweeting about soccer and former girlfriends.

Clarifying a Purpose

At one time, strategy did not change much from one year to the next. Market forces and business processes remained largely the same over the life of a company. With the increased speed and complexity of the digital age, however, organizations constantly face change. For continued success, even strategy has to adapt.

> The most important attribute of a strategy is how well people in the organization can breathe it into their daily actions

A digitally-ready organization must have both a clear purpose (e.g., why do we exist?) and the ability to effectively navigate toward that end. The availability and variety of digital tools appearing *outside* the organization pushes strategists to reconsider their methods for building and maintaining an effective *internal* organization. A shared vision ties together all of the activities, so the people who implement strategy are working in concert to support organizational goals.

Purpose is more than a statement of operational direction. It also encompasses several factors that determine how well employees can move within the organization toward that direction, including:

- the effectiveness of information sharing policies
- the level of control each person has over their choices
- the roles to which people are assigned
- the incentive structures

Most organizations already invest time and money defining strategic goals. This tends to happen early in the life of a company, then periodically as the business grows. Unfortunately, many of these official statements of strategic

1. Deliver WOW Through Service

2. Embrace and Drive Change

3. Create Fun and A Little Weirdness

4. Be Adventurous, Creative, and Open-Minded

5. Pursue Growth and Learning

6. Build Open and Honest Relationships With Communication

7. Build a Positive Team and Family Spirit

8. Do More With Less

9. Be Passionate and Determined

10. Be Humble

Figure 4.2
Zappos Family Core Values, explicitly defined to explain how the company develops their culture, brand, and business strategies.

direction end up as 50-page documents filled with vague, all-encompassing terms. In that form, even well-crafted strategic plans are difficult to disseminate to the people responsible for achieving those goals.

Ultimately, the most important attribute of a strategy is how well people in the organization can breathe it into their day-to-day actions[5]. In order for this to happen, the purpose of a company should be both *vivid* (easy for people to notice and remember) and *salient* (easy for people to apply to their own situation) for everyone in the organization [Ostrom, 2005; Gibbard, 1994, Jones 2001].

Zappos, the online company founded in 1999 to sell shoes, has a list of ten core values (see Figure 4.2, on previous page) known by everyone in the organization, from custodians to executives. These ten statements are short, specific and easy to remember (vivid), and it is easy for any person in the company to find them relevant (salient).

Employees understand the philosophy that each of these guiding principles represents. They are able to apply these values to the decisions they make when doing their jobs, regardless of their position in the organizational hierarchy. Any specific strategic goals crafted at Zappos (e.g., target sales for the quarter) become more achievable due to the shared purpose pervading the organization's culture.

5
Freek Vermeulen, an associate professor of strategic and international management at London Business School, writes, "A strategy only becomes a strategy if people in the organisation alter their behaviour as a result of it" [Vermeulen, 2011].

Seeking Alignment

To become digitally ready, an organization must align the actions it takes—acquiring new technology, investing resources to support adoption, fostering a fluent culture—with its stated purpose. Alignment creates both efficiency and clarity. It also improves agility, as individuals are better able to make decisions in the moment that help advance organizational goals.

As with learning, alignment is an ongoing process. Every shift outside the organization can prompt an adjustment on the inside. Technology distorts the culture of an organization, with innovations potentially so profound as to alter strategic goals. As new tools become available, policies and procedures must update to include their use. By standing still, organizations fail to keep step with change, appearing to observers to be stepping backward.

The consequences of misalignment can be costly. In an organization without much digital fluency, spending hundreds of thousands of dollars on high-end software may prove a bad decision. Unless the tool matches their abilities, people asked to use that system will struggle to implement it, resulting in limited benefit toward the company's stated purpose. Worse, misaligned people could make tactical mistakes during use from which they are ill-equipped to recover. These gaffes may be small (e.g., propagating irrelevant information) or huge (e.g., accidentally leaking company secrets).

A mark of digital readiness is when an organization is able to maintain alignment in the face of change. This focus requires adaptation, the ability to keep up with, get ahead of, and even to influence the change around you. The better an organization is at responding to shifts in its environment, the quicker it can focus on fulfilling its purpose.

Measuring Success

An organization filled with people who are digitally fluent—who are working toward a clear, common vision aligned with current tools and culture—has the best chance of success. To maintain that digital readiness, however, it is important to understand and communicate where the company is on that journey.

> **Strategic success is when your expected outcome matches the actual outcome.**

It seems straightforward, but *success* is complicated.

Conventional wisdom equates success with the acquisition of rewards and honors, or simply a happy ending to a journey. That fuzzy definition isn't practical enough to be of much use to an organization. It is difficult to communicate a shared purpose and progress made toward goals by adopting an *I'll know it when I see it* attitude.

One way to think of strategic success is as a pairing of two outcomes. The first outcome is what you want to happen—an organization applies its resources to a purpose with a desired result in mind. The second outcome is what actually does happen, the consequence of actions taken. When these two outcomes match, success occurs.

Our working definition is:

> *Strategic success is when your expected outcome matches the actual outcome.*[6]

The more fluent an organization is about preparing for an expected outcome, the better the chance they will get it. The complication is that no one can dictate

[6] Unexpected positive outcomes can and do happen to both people and organizations. We are not including those sorts of events in our definition of success, though, because the focus of this book is on what you can do to improve digital fluency, not the benefits of serendipity.

the outcome on their own, especially in a fast, complex digital world.

Even well-designed tools are appropriated by their users in new ways. Marketing efforts get derailed by negative reactions that gain social momentum. These kinds of external forces impact the results. People largely agree that use of digital media should improve the odds for success, however fuzzy the concept.

To communicate whether an effort is successful, the outcome must be easy to analyze. Whether a result is positive depends on what measures an organization associates with success. If success is defined as reaching $1 million in quarterly sales, then making $1.2 million could be considered an achievement. If success is improved client satisfaction, then a jump in customer ratings is declared a victory.

Organizations are also concerned with what it took to *gain* that success. If the cost of that $1.2 million included $4 million in manufacturing and marketing, for example, then the effort is a financial loss. Similarly, if an organization has to compromise its core values and ethics to improve customer satisfaction, then any gains in those scores may be overwhelmed by damage to its reputation and to trust in other areas of the company.

There is no universal formula to determine the future ROI of digital media.

Leaders trying to incorporate anticipated benefits of digital tools into their strategy often do so before using the technology. They are therefore ill-equipped to answer important questions about how much of an investment it will take to achieve success, and whether the return will be worth that investment.

There is no universal formula to determine the future ROI of digital media, as helpful as one might be. Each organization must understand its current and future situations well enough to define success within its own context. By reasoning through the issues that arise, an organization can uncover its most effective measures.

Two Mistakes to Avoid

Before we explore what measures organizations could attach to success, we need to emphasize two things *not* to do.

The first common mistake is expecting that success for one organization is the model for success in all organizations. The assumption of one-size-fits-all solutions does not take into account the dependencies between individuals, the organization, and the unique context in which they interact. These elements must work together to create success.

In a digitally ready organization with a digitally fluent workforce, the widespread use of a collaboration platform (e.g., Salesforce Chatter) may yield a big return on investment. On the other hand, the same platform introduced to literate employees in an organization lacking a clear purpose would likely yield little benefit, even if both organizations produced the same things for the same market.

The second common mistake is assuming the ROI from using digital media is based only on financial profit. The bottom line is critical for an organization to consider, but not all valuable activities lead directly to profit.

In 2004, Robert Kaplan and Dave Norton pointed out that none of an organization's intangible assets[7]—the things that

7
Robert Kaplan, a Harvard professor and member of the Accounting Hall of Fame, is credited with co-author Dave Norton with developing the Balanced Scorecard, a strategic performance methodology widely used by businesses around the world. Intangible assets include things like skills, talent and knowledge, information technology, culture, leadership, and alignment.

are not directly measured by the organization's financial system—can be measured independently of each other [McAfee, 2009]:

> Intangible assets such as knowledge and technology seldom have a direct impact on financial outcomes such as increased revenues, lowered costs, and higher profits. Improvements in intangible assets affect financial outcomes through chains of cause-and-effect relationships.

Metrics should strive to identify benefits most relevant to your particular organization.

The impact of digital technology is a complex, interconnected phenomenon with many paths leading to success. As a result, there are many kinds of value that should be sought to make digital initiatives successful.

A Different ROI

When trying to decide whether the use of digital technology is worth the effort, evaluation calls for a broad approach. To determine success, metrics should strive to identify benefits most relevant to a particular organization.

Norton and Kaplan's take on value creation, from their book *Strategy Maps* [Norton and Kaplan, 2004], provides a helpful perspective on ROI. We particularly like four core concepts from their work, adapted and applied here to digital media:

Potential is important

The financial cost of digital media is a poor estimate of its value to the organization. Like other processes (e.g., statistical quality control methods), the use of digital media creates potential value, not market value. It allows people to do things in ways they previously couldn't.

Financial success is created indirectly

The use of digital media occasionally yields direct profit. More often, its use produces other benefits further up the value chain. For example, an organization might encourage the use of Google+ to improve collaboration. In turn, collaboration fosters innovation, elevates product quality, and may then lead to more loyal customers. Sales and profit are built on that foundation.

Clear value requires a clear purpose

If the use of digital media is not directed toward an organization's goals, it is unlikely to produce value for that organization. Online engagement with customers may lead to more clicks to the company website, but for a company that doesn't rely on the website for its business, the value gained by using digital media may be misplaced.

Digital tools are bundled

Digital tools seldom create value by themselves. They cannot be isolated from organizational context. Tools create value when they are coordinated with other assets, both tangible (easy to measure against high-level goals) and intangible (value supporting tangible assets). The use of an internal microblog like Yammer, for example, is more effective when it is combined with a diverse workforce, up-to-date hardware, and an institutional goal to increase knowledge. Maximum value is created when assets are aligned with each other and with a shared purpose.

For success to occur within an organization, the individual digital fluency of everyone from the C-suite to the part-time worker must be enhanced. This is accomplished by expanding access to appropriate tools and resources, cultivating a healthy culture for collaboration, and providing a shared set of strategies to benefit the organization[8]. Everyone should know what success looks like and the proper ways to measure it.

8
In future publications, we will dive deep into the specifics of these organization-level mechanisms not fully covered in this chapter. In Chapter 5, we return to our discussion of individual digital fluency, suggesting specific steps you can take today to begin to develop it.

By this point, we hope you are as convinced as we are that the development and maintenance of your digital fluency is one of the most important things you can do for yourself and your organization. It is as fundamental as reading and writing.

Moving beyond digital literacy impacts how successful you may be in your work, your community, and even in your personal relationships.

In the final chapter, we provide some practical ideas and specific activities that you can try to build and maintain your digital fluency. Give them a try. Share them with others. Use them to plant the seeds of your own methods for communicating, creating, and learning.

Want to find out how digitally fluent you are?

Take a short survey at:
mydigitalfluency.socialens.com

Rewind

What we've covered so far

Most of what you are capable of doing now remains critical to success in the digital age.

Skills are the mental, verbal or physical manipulation of data or objects.

Knowledge helps people make beneficial decisions.

Our mindset shapes how our abilities might be applied to a situation.

There are four stages of learning: Anti-Literacy, Pre-Literacy, Literacy, and Fluency.

Anti-Literacy and Literacy are ripe for stagnation, since people in those stages tend not to value change.

Fluency gives a person the best possible chance of succeeding, given what is within his control.

First-hand experience is the best way to develop the abilities that lead to fluency.

Strategic success is when your expected outcome matches the actual outcome.

Metrics should strive to identify benefits most relevant to your organization.

"Sharing knowledge occurs when people are genuinely interested in helping one another develop new capacities for action; it is about creating learning processes."

—PETER SENGE

Changes Look Good

It's 8:15 a.m. Sam waits for his laptop to finish reconnecting to the wi-fi network at his company. The previous day's blogs and tweets are frozen on the screen, waiting for fresh information to replace them. Suddenly, it all springs to life, with scrolling posts and alerts flooding his screen.

In his newsfeed—a vertical stream of short headlines—he finds a link to a project some colleagues are working on. He clicks, automatically opening a browser to the revision a team member made to a wiki page. Sam notes the timestamp: 4:23a. The author, Sarah, is half done with her London day by now.

Below the wiki page are two comments. The first, posted at 4:30a by Daichi, states: "Changes look good to me. Glad to catch this before going home to Tokyo." David, based in Chicago, posted the second comment just a few minutes ago.

Sam opens up Skype, a voice and chat service, and looks for David's name. The green checkmark indicates, along with his recent comment, that he is probably available for a quick chat. There was a time when Sam would have to wait until 10:30 a.m. and hope that David would be available for a phone call, but today he types a quick question and waits. After a minute or two, it becomes clear there won't be an immediate response, but Sam is comforted knowing the conversation is there for David when he is free, in the communication channel he prefers. David rarely answers email anymore.

It is an adjustment for their team to be able to work this way. Each member of the team, despite being scattered around the world, has come to understand what kinds of tools are at their disposal and how they are most effective. Sarah led the way to help transform how the team works together, reflecting on their past frustrations and getting everyone on board to try some new digital tools. Sometimes the experiments failed, but Sam is happy his mornings feel more productive. That translates to less pressure to stay late and take time away from his kids.

He clicks a button to open up the wiki page for editing, and begins typing.

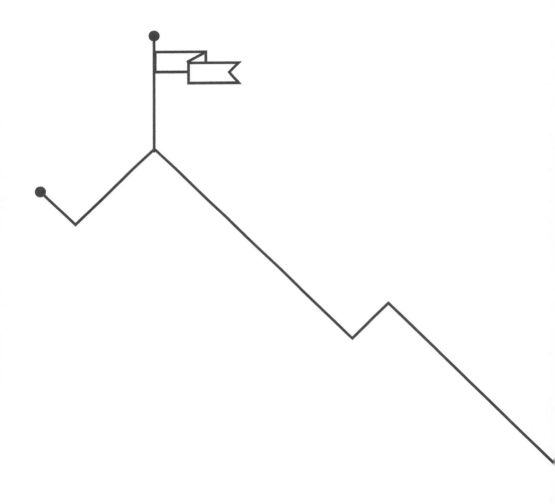

DIGITAL FLUENCY

5

Starting Today

Begin to build and maintain digital fluency with a few key exercises

In this chapter, we will provide you with some practical tips and simple exercises that you can practice today to begin your journey to digital fluency. These activities are designed to require minimal investment of time to gain hands-on experience with the range of abilities needed for success in the digital age. Wherever you are in the learning process (see Chapter 3), challenge your assumptions about digital media and connect these assignments with your own work context.

Before you dive into the exercises, though, there are two things you should do to prepare.

Set a Clear Goal

No one gets far on a trip if they don't know where they are going. A traveler without a destination will wander aimlessly, and one without a map may have difficulty finding that destination. Your organization may have specific goals that are vivid and relevant to you and your colleagues. If so, you can use this shared vision as your context for the exercises.

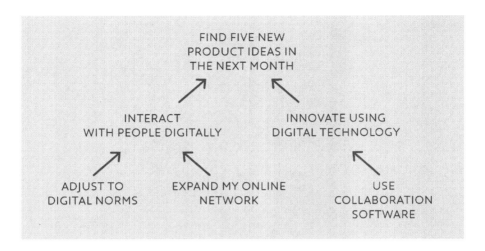

FIND FIVE NEW
PRODUCT IDEAS IN
THE NEXT MONTH

INTERACT
WITH PEOPLE DIGITALLY

INNOVATE USING
DIGITAL TECHNOLOGY

ADJUST TO
DIGITAL NORMS

EXPAND MY ONLINE
NETWORK

USE
COLLABORATION
SOFTWARE

Figure 5.1.
An example
of a simple
strategy map

1
The corporate
world is littered
with ambiguous
mission
statements and
40-page strategy
documents. These
forms of strategy
are either too
general or too
detailed to be
useful in day-to-day
decision making.
A good way to
test your existing
strategy to see if it
is vivid and salient
(see "Clarifying a
Purpose" in Chapter
4) is to map it
visually onto a
single page.

If your organization lacks clarity of purpose, specify a personal goal for developing digital fluency, such as: "Lessen my email load by 30 percent in four months," or "Spark three online discussions about our future in the next 30 days." This will allow you to practice decision-making and planning toward a clear end.

One way to do this is to draw a simple *strategy map,* a visual representation of goals and what is required to achieve those goals[1] (Figure 5.1). The bottom row of the map reflects the specific abilities—built from knowledge, skills and mindsets—that you might work on to develop aspects of your digital fluency. These feed the types of actions you can take (the second row). Everything should support your main goal, at the top of the map.

Draw your specific actions from this hierarchy. If your primary goal is improving company morale, the use of digital technology may help you to collaborate with other people. Start developing your ability to interact with others through digital tools, experimenting with ones you don't already use. If you want to lessen information overload, work on your ability to recognize relevant information, perhaps by signing up for a filtering tool (e.g., CoTweet). If your department has established a target of five new product ideas in the next month, your ability to innovate may be helped by submitting ideas to online communities for feedback.

A strategy map acts as a touchstone: *Will doing this help me reach my goal?* At every level, the focus is on doing the things that best support what you want to accomplish.

Measure Your Progress

The bane of family trips is the inevitable question, asked in the car on a long drive: "Are we there yet?" It is posed in large part because the kids in the backseat do not have access to the same information as the driver, whose odometer and map provide valuable feedback about the journey's progress.

Humans accomplish their goals more efficiently, and with more joy, when they know how far they have come, and how much further they have to go.

Researchers Teresa Amabile and Steven Kramer examined what motivated people to do good work[2]. For three years, the researchers studied more than 12,000 diary entries logged by knowledge workers [Amabile and Kramer, 2007], looking at the factors that might contribute to engagement with their jobs and doing meaningful work. When they compared the best days to the worst, Amabile and Kramer found that the biggest differentiator was understanding the progress made in their work.

2
In their recent book The Progress Principle, Amabile and Kramer looked closely at employees' perceptions, emotions and motivation levels, something they call *the inner work life*, across several dimensions of performance.

As you work toward developing digital fluency, it is important to map out goals to make your efforts meaningful. It is important to, in some way, measure the progress made toward achieving those goals.

Metrics can be as simple or complex as is necessary, and can be either quantitative (tallying the number of things) or qualitative (understanding the value of things). In our example strategy map where the goal is to generate five quality ideas (see Figure 5.1), you might take a few minutes each month to measure success by asking a friend for a critique or counting how many ideas you produced.

A commitment to regularly checking progress will help sustain efforts to meet a goal. It will provide you the feedback you need to modify your methods, should the results prove undesirable. Knowing your progress also keeps you engaged with what you are doing.

Improve Your Abilities

As we discussed in Chapter 2, developing the raw materials of fluency—the mix of knowledge, skills, and mindset that affect your ability to succeed—is an ongoing learning process. The situation around you is constantly changing at an ever-increasing rate and with greater and greater complexity. For you to maintain or increase your digital fluency, it is vital to attend to these things regularly.

There are two different dimensions you can consider when improving your ability to adapt to change: the depth and the diversity of what you know, do, and believe.

Deepen Your Insights
Surface knowledge and rudimentary skills can only get you so far. The more you immerse yourself in understanding the things you can do, the better you will comprehend the powers and limitations of your abilities.

A woman who multitasks with multiple devices, for example, may also be aware of the times when she needs to close down potential distractions and focus. The man who has mastered the art of creating viral videos will understand that some part of its popularity is beyond his control. A deep dive into the forces at work during these activities will reveal new insights about how you can get more out of that ability.

Diversify Your Toolbox

Being able to do one thing extremely well could have a down side: If that is the only experience you have, you likely have a narrow view of how the world works. The wider your range of abilities, the more perspectives you can bring to bear on a situation.

If you are skilled at using both mobile devices and the virtual world SecondLife, you might be able to leverage both platforms to train large groups of people more effectively. If you can motivate others and deal with massive amounts of information, it will be easier for you to switch between these tactics when introducing social media monitoring tools to your team. Developing a diverse range of abilities creates new ways to approach your goals and gives you the agility required to make quick adjustments, should your initial attempts fail.

The following twelve exercises are designed to help you develop the twelve types of abilities listed in Chapter 3. Each five- to ten-minute exercise explains how it connects to a particular ability group and lists some circumstances when this skill might be useful. For these exercises, you will need Internet access, as well as an account on at least one social network, like Facebook, Twitter, or Google+. As with any learning process, regular practice can eventually work itself into a daily routine.

Iter-8-tion

Better your

- Innovation
- Interactions

Success could be

- 2 people respond to you
- you like your last idea better than the first

Practice generating ideas quickly, choosing the best of several to share publicly.

At first glance, play may seem like a frivolous skill for a professional, but it is critical to success in the digital age. The more able people are to make quick corrections to small experiments, the better their organizations will be in adapting to a fast-moving world. Especially for a perfectionist, it can be difficult to share incomplete thoughts or casual interests with other people. This is particularly true when using digital media, where an electronic record likely will exist beyond that moment. Digital fluency requires us to be able to share information, especially when we are trying to get answers to a question or work on solutions to a problem.

1. Write down 4 short ideas you have for improving your life. Throw them all away and write 4 more (e.g., *Eat more vegetables*). **2 minutes**

2. Log into your favorite social network and post one idea to your friends, fans, or followers (e.g., *Should I eat more vegetables? What do you guys think?*). **1 minutes**

3. An hour later, check for responses. Use any feedback along with your own reflection to alter the way you re-share your idea (e.g., *Since Joe says green vegetables are healthiest, I am thinking of eating more green vegetables.*). **2 minutes**

Me, Myself & I

Change your current profile picture to a cartoon picture that represents your actual appearance.

Every day, we manage how we present ourselves to others. With or without computers, we consider the roles we must play, how we want to be perceived, and how our communication will be best understood. The ability to adopt identities that are appropriate to one community or the next is a important part of digital fluency. Being able to move fluidly and effectively between these versions of yourself can help you when you are trying to decide what actions are ethical in a given context, and how best to interact with co-workers, family or strangers. .

1.	Use an online tool (see Resources at right) to create an avatar of yourself. Try to make the picture look as much like you as possible, given whatever options the tool allows. Save your new avatar to your desktop.	8 minutes
2.	Log into your favorite social network account (e.g., Facebook) and change your current profile picture to your new avatar.	1 minute
3.	Post a message to your online friends using that social network site. Ask them what they think of your new profile picture (e.g., *I just changed my avatar. Does it look like me?*).	1 minute

Better your

- Interactions

Success could be

- A friend suggests an improvement
- More people like the new avatar than not

Resources:

southparkstudios.com/avatar

unique.rasterboy.com

amctv.com/madmenyourself

simpsonsmovie.com

NOTE:

This exercise requires that you have already registered for an account on a social network website

Traffic Cop

Experiment with a NetLogo traffic simulation tool to understand which decisions best keep cars moving.

Better your

- Information Handling
- Inspiration
- Innovation

Success could be

- A discussion about modeling business practices becomes a project
- You gain one key insight about the dynamics of traffic jams

Resources:

ccl.northwestern.
edu/netlogo/models

A smartphone video camera can be used to create a prototype for a product use case; Virtual environments like SecondLife can become playgrounds for serious business. The low cost of computing power makes it easier than ever to use digital tools to gain insights about cultural trends, customer sentiment, and company performance. The digital age has given rise to simulations, abstracting the real world to help analyze, predict, or prototype what might occur. Being able to interpret, manipulate and create simulations can help you quickly understand complexities in the world—but only for people with the ability to use these tools fluently.

1. Visit Northwestern University's NetLogo project site and run the "Traffic Grid" simulation program (see Resources at left).   1 minute

2. Click "Setup" and then "Go" to run the model, which simulates the flow of cars through a grid of intersections controlled with stoplights. After noting the results, adjust the settings and run it again.   5 minutes

3. Identify one process in your organization that could be modeled with NetLogo to better understand how to make it more efficient. (e.g., *Time to complete client jobs*).   2 minutes

Mashing Media

Experience ways data and digital media are combined together to create something new.

In the digital age, it is easier than ever to combine other people's artifacts, data, and software into something new. Meaningful and persuasive content can be created by remixing existing work that was originally created for a different purpose. Appropriation of someone else's content involves understanding the complex legal and economic realities of different licensing options, ranging from stringent copyright to highly-permissive Creative Commons agreements. Many companies share their data and functionality through Application Programming Interfaces (APIs) that invite re-use. The ability to do this well can generate new ideas, improve efficiency, and even help others envision a better future.

Better your

- Information Handling
- Innovation

Success could be

- Enjoying the mashups you viewed
- Getting one mashup idea that could benefit your company

Resources:

thru-you.com
flood.firetree.net
creativecommons.org

1. Visit Thru-You (see Resources at right) to see an example of a video mashup. Kutiman recombined hundreds of amateur videos by musicians to create new music. — 4 minutes

2. Visit the Firetree Flood Map to see an example of a data mashup. This involves mixing Google Maps and NASA data. — 4 minutes

3. Think about data or content that your organization has that could be combined to create new value (e.g., *Customer location data and national news stories*). — 2 minutes

Focus Focus

Better your

- Information Handling
- Innovation

Success could be

- You check the Twitter stream only six times in an hour
- You laugh at least once by what you encounter while checking Twitter

Resources:

search.twitter.com

Launch a Twitter search and check it several times while working on something else.

Each of us have choices for what we could do in any given moment. Right now, for example, you could check your Facebook profile, call a colleague to check on a current project, or start typing an important document. You could also try to do them all at the same time. Multitasking is about making smart choices—based on your own abilities, priorities, and the context—about when to shift focus between activities with competing value.

1. Open Twitter Search in a web browser (see Resources at left) and enter a search term about which you are interested (e.g., *football*). As people post about that topic, Twitter will update the results page automatically. Resize the browser window so that you can see it running on your computer while you work.   1 minute

2. If you get too much information, try refining the search (e.g., *Chicago football*) to be more specific. If you get too little information, broaden the topic (e.g., *sports*).   1 minute

3. Check the search window every 10 minutes, clicking on the "new tweets" bar at the top of the stream. Make a short list of the most interesting things you learned from these tweets.   3 minutes

Machine Friends

Compare the results from Google alerts for you and your company.

From the first time humans marked a cave wall to keep track of the number of buffalo killed, we have been using technologies to expand our mental capacities. We record memories and thoughts in journals, solve long math problems with a calculator, and plan our near futures through Google Calendar. New technologies are arriving daily that continue this trend. Using them wisely can make us and our organizations smarter with information. Distributed cognition is the ability to interact meaningfully with these tools to augment what our brain can remember.

Better your

- Information Handling
- Interaction
- Innovation

Success could be

- Find five examples of others reporting on your company
- Understand one important distinction between your personal and organizational identities

Resources:

google.com/alerts

1. Visit Google's alerts form (see Resources at right) and create an alert for your name (e.g., *Christian Briggs*). Configure the alert to send a notices to your email account "As-it-happens."   —   1 minute

2. Create a second alert for your company name (e.g., *SociaLens*), duplicating the rest of the settings from the previous alert.   —   1 minute

3. A few days later, compare the notifications you receive from each alert. Discuss with a friend any differences you observed in how those two identities are perceived on the Internet.   —   3 minutes

Smarter Together

Better your

- Information Handling
- Interactions
- Involvement
- Innovation

Success could be

- Five people answer your question in the first 60 minutes
- You feel supported by others who answered in the same way as you

Resources:

facebook.com

Ask a question of your friends on Facebook, and use their responses to start an online discussion.

Our fast, complex world affords us unprecedented opportunities to efficiently coordinate our knowledge and actions. We can do so as easily with two people as two thousand. Wikipedia is recognized as one of the largest examples of collective intelligence, but this is also true of the World of Warcraft Wiki (WoWWiki), too, which currently has over 93,000 pages of user-contributed information about the game and how to play it. The ability to understand and use digital technologies to solicit help in furthering goals makes everyone smarter.

1. Log into your Facebook account. At the top of the page, click "Ask Question," and type something you would like answered by your friends (e.g., *What is the best way you've found to fight information overload?*).

   2 minutes

2. Check back later for responses. Facebook offers a number of notification methods, if you want to respond in real-time.

   1 minute

3. Engage commenters about their answers to your question. Make use of Facebook's "Like" button to endorse a particular comment, or extend it into a discussion thread by sharing a relevant personal experience, providing an additional resource, or asking a follow-up question.

   7 minutes

Judge Cred

Compare web search and crowdsourcing as methods of verifying suspect information.

Better your

- Information Handling

The ability to evaluate the reliability and credibility of different sources is critical as the flow of information speeds up. Collective intelligence and individual creativity can amplify misinformation, spreading questionable data through networks of people and machines. To understand which parts are credible requires a new sense of context, quickly evaluating where it came from and when to seek additional verification. Judgment enables a person to efficiently locate and filter out unreliable information, and to focus on information that will help the organization.

Success could be

- Crafting a keyword search that gets an answer in the fewest number of clicks
- Reconnecting with a friend to whom you seldom talk

Resources:

1. Open up a web browser and use your default search engine to confirm or refute the following claims:

   a) Ivory Soap's ability to float was a result of an accident

   b) Michael Jordan was cut from his high school basketball team

   5 minutes

   google.com

2. Pose these to claims to your network of online friends, and ask them whether it is true.

   2 minutes

3. Compare the results of the two methods of verifying information. Share any differences you find interesting with your online friends.

   3 minutes

Media Messages

Navigate from print to online news, noting how each medium offers the reader something unique.

Better your

- Information Handling

Success could be

- Reading an interesting article found after following one or more additional links
- Using a smartphone to launch a website from a QR code

As the number of available information channels increases, so does the likelihood that a conversation or a story will jump from one form of media to another. A conversation with a colleague might start on the phone during a drive to a client site, and then continue as an online chat later that day, or a face-to-face meeting when she gets back to the office. Many print magazine advertisements now include QR codes (a two-dimensional barcode) that enable people to take a photo of the advertisement with a smartphone and launch a website. Transmedia Navigation gives a person the ability to both craft and experience these sorts of stories.

1. From your favorite major newspaper or magazine and find a printed article that references the online version.

   3 minutes

2. Visit the online version of the story, and list the ways that the online version is different. Consider the writing style, advertisements, commenting and sharing features.

   4 minutes

3. Click on a link embedded in the online article. Use any of the online sharing options you encounter (e.g., *email to a friend*) so send yourself a link to the story.

   2 minutes

Info Networks

Ask your online friends to help research a new topic suggested by an offline colleague who knows it well.

In the digital age, it is imperative that a person understand how data moves through a network. The structure of a network impacts how information is passed from person to person, and from community to community. Participating in information networks can be overwhelming, so it is vital that people learn what to do with high volume or a lack of relevance. Even finding the tools created to help one manage information overload can be a daunting task, given their number and similarity. The ability to efficiently search for, synthesize, and disseminate digital information is one of the biggest parts of digital fluency.

Better your

- Information Handling
- Inspiration
- Involvement

Success could be

- You learn something interesting about an offline colleague that could improve future communication
- Half of the friends participating in this exercise bring some new information to the group

1. Ask an offline colleague (i.e., in person) to select a topic about which they know a great deal, but you do not.   2 minutes

2. Ask your online friends to spend exactly 3 minutes gathering as much information as possible on this topic, relying on both past experiences and new searches to complete the task. (You search, too.)   3 minutes

3. Report the aggregated information to your colleague and ask for a critique of its value.   5 minutes

Community Explorer

Join a new online community and post to that website in a manner that matches the way they communicate.

Better your

- Interactions
- Inspiration
- Involvement

Success could be

- At least one person responds to your comment
- A week after this exercise, you are actively participating in this new community

Resources:

digg.com
forums.oxygen.com
boards.fool.com
reddit.com

On a standard desktop computer, in addition to running production software (e.g., Microsoft Word), most of us have a few windows open simultaneously, connected to completely different communities, like Gmail, Facebook, or an online support forum. Often, these communities have different legal restrictions, ways of interacting, degree of formality, and other member behaviors. A fluent person can rapidly switch between one community and the next, quickly negotiating the space between and adapting to the rules and norms of each. This ability is especially critical when interacting with people outside of an organization.

1. Set up an account on a community website that you have never visited before (see Resources at left for suggestions). — 3 minutes

2. Quickly browse the existing content contributed by other members (e.g., *forum posts*). Write down at least one thing about this community that is different from what you are used to (e.g., *level of sarcasm*). — 3 minutes

3. Using whatever tools this website allows, respond to someone else's content in a manner consistent with the community norm you wrote down. — 4 minutes

Pictures in Clouds

Generate word clouds for two political blogs, and compare the word usage in both.

In the world of "Big Data," making visual sense of massive amounts of information becomes extremely important. Fluent people are also capable of finding patterns, identifying trends and mining key insights from large data sets. Visualization abilities allow a person to communicate highly-complex concepts to others in efficient and compelling ways, both by creating information graphics and being able to reference and explain the visualizations of others. Such crafted images have become a key way we cope with a lot of information and make sense of the complexity of our environment.

1. Arrange two separate browser windows side-by-side and visit Wordle's create form in each (see Resources at right).   1 minute

2. The second text box from the top of the Wordle create form allows you to enter the URL for a website. In the first browser window, enter the URL for The Foundry, a conservative blog by The Heritage Foundation. In the second window, enter the URL for Daily Kos, a liberal blog (see Resources at right) .   2 minutes

3. Compare the two Wordle visualizations. List a few words that are most common to each.   5 minutes

Better your

- Information Handling
- Innovation
- Imagination

Success could be

- Changing the presentation of these word clouds to better highlight the distinctions.
- Repeating this exercise each week reveals an insight about how these two groups evolve their conversations

Resources:

wordle.net/create

blog.heritage.com

feeds.dailykos.com/dailykos/index.xml

"I cannot help fearing that men may reach a point where they look on every new theory as a danger, every innovation as a toilsome trouble, every social advance as a first step toward revolution, and that they may absolutely refuse to move at all."

—ALEXIS DE TOCQUEVILLE

Digital Fluency in The Wild

The deadline looms for Georgia. Her editor at the *Boston Globe* doesn't like to give extensions, but the cub reporter knows she needs a few more quotes for her story. The last two stops on her tour of area businesses are a machinery shop and a training consultant.

Georgia is writing about how businesses have dealt with life in the digital age. Some of her interviews have uncovered horror stories about failed adoption of software or underwhelming results, but there are a number of companies in town who have had some success in this area. Georgia is in the lobby of one of these places, Superior Machinery, run by a woman who tripled the size of the company since taking over for her late husband a little over half a decade ago.

A distinguished woman descends a staircase. She carries a leather briefcase as she moves toward the reporter. Georgia notices sneakers on her feet.

"Welcome to Superior," Louise says, extending a free hand to Georgia. "I thought we could meet in my office."

Louise moves past Georgia for the lobby door, holding it open for the reporter to follow. Noticing the confused look on the face staring back at her, Louise explains: "I do much of my work at the cafe around the corner."

* * * * * *

This gingerbread cookie is fantastic, Georgia thinks to herself as she takes another bite. The conversation with Louise has been casual, but quite informative.

The leather binder is open in front of Louise, who glances at it occasionally as they talk. It is a minor distraction for Georgia, but no more than the cookie or the bustle of activity all around them. Louise says she likes the energy in this room as much as the tea she is drinking, and several of her employees often come to this neighborhood cafe for meetings.

Adeptly, Louise turns the tablet toward Georgia to show her the device. On the screen, a video is paused showing three people on a conference panel. "It's the Six Sigma conference in California," Louise explains. She points a finger at the man on the left end. "That's Michael, one of our product development guys. When he gave the talk yesterday, we had it on our big screen in the office."

With a prod from Georgia, Louise plays some of the video. Michael is talking about how Superior Machinery has used digital technology to carry the voice of their customer (VOC) into their manufacturing process, without surveys or expensive on-site visits. Video, microblogging, and other forms of digital collaboration have saved Superior money while improving their customer satisfaction scores. Everything moves a bit faster than it used to, but that doesn't translate into more information as much as greater convenience.

"Our teams are energized by all of this," Louise says. When Georgia asks why, Louise pauses. "I'm not completely sure. We're just more focused when we talk to clients."

Louise sips her tea. She is quiet as she remembers that cab ride, long ago, and ridiculing people for how much their devices seemed to take over their lives. Now, with many months of her own experiences, she sees this tablet on the table as a tool that helps her do what she's always done: make and sell her product.

As a CEO, her managers' meetings still include statistics for productivity and profitability, but Louise also feels more intimately aware of the emotional state of both her employees and of her customers. Just two days earlier, Louise noticed a conspicuous lack of chatter—a new word she uses for people using digital tools—coming from one of her key employees. When she saw him in the break room, Louise asked if he was okay. He was not, and they were able to have an impromptu discussion right there about an important issue that had been bothering him.

"I don't use Twitter," Louise tells Georgia, "but I'm glad we have people at Superior who do."

* * * * * *

Georgia now sits in a comfortable office. On the wall is a framed picture of three kids. A moment later, it changes to a photo of a man with his family at Disneyworld. Georgia has been watching images change in this way for a few minutes, as she waits for her last interview to begin.

A glass of water is extended in front of Georgia. She turns her attention from the digital frame to see the man from the picture, Sam, offering her a drink. "That last one was from Christmas," he explains, nodding at the frame. "A lot has changed since then."

Georgia is excited to talk to Sam because his company is updating their internal social network today to allow some external clients to participate, something that is the product of many months of wrangling and experimentation. Forty-five clients from 32 partner organizations will now be able to comment on projects and help craft some of the learning plans the firm uses in their education initiatives.

"Sarah, from our London office, thought it would help us be more responsive and relevant to our clients," Sam recalls. "Things are moving faster for them, too, and we want to keep pace."

Sam picks up a book from a nearby shelf and hands it to Georgia. The cover reads *The Power of Co-Creation*, by Venkat Ramaswamy and Francis Gouillart. "Sarah got us all hooked on this idea of involving the people we serve in defining their own services. We're trying to become a 'co-creation platform.'" Sam chuckles. He still finds the term odd to say out loud.

The biggest challenge in the coming weeks, Sam admits, will be managing employee comfort levels with this kind of transparency. Particularly with some of the veterans in the company, exposing the company's process—where mistakes are common as they work to build their programs—seems dangerous. One writer on Sam's team is convinced that letting clients see the unpolished material will frighten them away and ruin the company's good reputation. Even after helping run short digital fluency workshops, Sam doesn't know if this employee and others like him will ever be comfortable with co-creation.

Sam is uneasy, too. He tells Georgia about mistakes he has made while using tools like Twitter, Facebook, and the company wiki. After the gaffes, he wanted to stop using these tools. It never feels good to make a mistake. With some coaching from peers, though, he worked through the errors and learned. "That's what we do, after all," Sam says. "Social media is no place for perfectionists, but it is wonderful for learners."

As Georgia scribbles notes on a pad of paper, Sam notices the logo on the coffee cup she had placed on his desk. "Carmine's cookies are great, aren't they?" he asks. Georgia stops writing and looks at him curiously, wondering how he knew she had been there today. "She told me the secret ingredient, you know."

"What is it?" asks Georgia, remembering the taste.

Sam leans back and smiles. "I've learned just because you have the information, doesn't mean it's meant to share. You'll have to ask Carmine yourself."

A low-key chirp comes from the smartphone on Sam's desk. He glances at the screen, which reads: "Need ... cookies ... ." The message is from his youngest daughter, 7, whose bright face appears next to the words. At that age, Sam's only options to reach out to his own dad at work were the phone or maybe the post office . The new digital toys seem so natural to her, but Sam believes that is because she is open to trying it out. His daughter sees only the possibilities.

While Georgia continues the Q&A, Sam is drawn to the digital picture frame. He watches things change before his eyes.

Becoming Digitally Fluent

BY GEORGIA ROWLAND
Boston Globe

Eighteen months ago, Sam and Louise crossed paths in Davis Square. Since then, both have seen many changes in themselves, their colleagues and organizations, and the world at large, all due to the pervasiveness of digital technology.

Though their journeys are far from over, both have reached some level of comfort with digital technology that allows them to adapt to change, learn new things, and even nudge their companies in more positive directions.

CONTINUED ON PAGE 2

It has not been easy, of course. Like commuters trying to keep their balance on an accelerating subway train, both were knocked a little off balance at times, as they adjusted to the speed and complexity of this new world. They feel more comfortable now, but getting to this point was work.

To start their journey, both Sam and Louise invested time in shifting their perspectives. As perfectionists—Sam as a communicator and Louise as a manager—they struggled to throttle down their fear of an incomplete or uncertain situation in order to develop an ability to share. They added some new skills, too: rooting out false information, adjusting quickly to evolving protocols in online communities, and trusting others to work toward a shared vision of their respective companies.

Today, Louise is better able to connect with her Superior Machinery customers and her company data, even as she finds herself less connected to her desk. Sam and his colleagues at One Mind are working faster across several global locations, fostering wider collaboration throughout the company and improving course offerings to executives around the world.

As she made this transition, Louise recognized her company's strategy was going to have to change, too. She met with her HR Director and crafted a new technology policy which allowed the use of digital devices on the manufacturing floor and unfettered Internet access, two things she would have rejected the previous year. Sam arranged for "digital fluency" coaching sessions, to help align use of new collaboration software with the existing goals of his company. They credit some of their recent success with this kind of preparation for change.

"One member of our board started peppering us with questions about the return for stakeholders," Sam recalls. "I asked him how much money he made golfing with the executive team. Sometimes, the investment is in a relationship. Not every action leads directly to a sale."

The large monitors streaming news and employee updates, or the participatory practices they have adopted to include customer input, doesn't mean Louise and Sam are done learning. They insist they continue to face change each day, and they are still working to keep pace. It is the same kind of situation they faced 18 months ago, only now both Sam and Louise have the digital fluency to adapt.

Extended Bibliography

1. Amabile, T., and Kramer, S. (2011). *The Progress Principle*. Harvard Business Press.

2. Amabile, T.M., and Kramer, S.J. (2007). Inner Work Life: Understanding the Subtext of Business Performance, *Harvard Business Review*. Retrieved on May 1, 2007 from http://hbr.org/product/inner-work-life-understanding-the-subtext-of-busin/an/ R0705D-PDF-ENG

3. Argyris, C., and Schön, D. (1978) *Organizational learning: A theory of action perspective,* Reading, Mass: Addison Wesley.

4. Argyris, C., and Schön, D. (1974). *Theory in Practice. Increasing professional effectiveness*. San Francisco, CA: Jossey-Bass.

5. Assi, R. (2010). Learn Social Media by Example: Skittles Steals the Social Media Rainbow, *ThoughtPick*. Retrieved on December 14, 2011 from http://blog. thoughtpick.com/2010/02/learn-social-media-by-example-skittles-steals-the-social-media-rainbow.html

6. Axon, S. (2010). Old Spice Sales Double With YouTube Campaign, *Mashable*. Retrieved on July 27, 2010 from http://mashable.com/2010/07/27/old-spice-sales

7. Ayers, C. (2009). Revenge is best served cold – on YouTube, *The Times* (London). Retrieved on July 22, 2009 from http://www.timesonline.co.uk/tol/comment/ columnists/chris_ayres/article6722407.ece

8. Bandura, A. (1977). *Social Learning Theory*. General Learning Press.

9. Bell, G. (2011). Women And Children First: Technology And Moral Panic, *Wall Street Journal* (blog). Retrieved on December 17, 2011 from http://blogs.wsj.com/tech-europe/2011/07/11/women-and-children-first-technology-and-moral-panic

10. Beniger, JR.(1986). *The control revolution: Technological and economic origins of the information society*. Harvard University Press.

11. Bernoff, J., and C. Li. (2008). *Groundswell: Winning in a world transformed by social technologies*. Boston: Harvard Business School Publishing.

12. Bolter, J.D., and Grusin, R. (2000). *Remediation: Understanding New Media*. The MIT Press.

13. Bardzell, J., Bolter, J., and Löwgren, J. (2010). Interaction criticism: three readings of an interaction design, and what they get us. *Interactions 17* (2), 32-37.

14. Briggs, C. (2008). The Tocqueville lens: Informing the design of the new township. In *Proceedings of the North American Computing and Philosophy Conference*.

15. Cairncross, F. (1995). The Death of Distance, *The Economist, 336*(7934).

16. Capell, K. (2009). When Skittles Met Twitter, *Bloomberg Businessweek*. Retrieved on 3/8/09 from http://www.businessweek.com/managing/content/mar2009/ca2009038_020385.htm

17. Carey, W.P. (2009). Zappos CEO Tony Hsieh: Customer focus key to record sales during retail slump, *Marketing and Services Leadership*. Retrieved on January 14, 2009 from http://knowledge.wpcarey.asu.edu/article.cfm?articleid=1736

18. Carroll, D. "Story" *Dave Carroll Music*. Retrieved on December 17, 2011 from http://www.davecarrollmusic.com/ubg/story/

19. Coase, R. H. (1937). The nature of the firm. *Economica, 386–405.*

20. Cisco Systems. (2011). *Connected World Technology Report*. Retrieved from http://www.cisco.com/en/US/netsol/ns1120/index.html

21. Cohen, N. (2009). Twitter on the Barricades: Six Lessons Learned, *New York Times*. (2009, June 20) [Blog post]. Retrieved on March 20, 2012 from http://www.nytimes.com/2009/06/21/weekinreview/21cohenweb.html

22. Cosby, B. (1987) *Himself.*

23. Daft, R.L., and Lengel, R.H. (1984). Information richness: A new approach to managerial behavior and organizational design. *Research in Organizational Behavior, 6,* 191-233.

24. Dawkins R. (1976). *The Selfish Gene.* New York: Oxford University Press.

25. Deming, W. E. (1985). Transformation of Western style of management, *Interfaces, 15* (3), 6-11.

26. Dreyfus, H.L., and Dreyfus, S.E. (1986). *Mind over machine: The power of human intuition and expertise in the age of the computer*, Oxford: Basil Blackwell.

27. Dreyfus, S.E., and Dreyfus, H.L. (1980). *A Five-stage model of the mental activities involved in directed skill acquisition.* Washington, DC: Storming Media.

28. Emery, D. (2010) . Whiteboard girl hoax fools thousands on net, *BBC News*. Retrieved on December 12, 2011 from http://www.bbc.co.uk/news/technology-10942340.

29. ESPN social networking policy, (2011). Retrieved on December 17, 2011 from http://frontrow.espn.go.com/wp-content/uploads/2011/08/social-networking-v2-2011.pdf

30. ETS. (2002). Succeeding in the 21st century: What higher education must do to address the gap in information and communication technology proficiencies, ETS. Retrieved on December 17, 2011 from http://www.ets.org/Media/Tests/Information_and_Communication_Technology_Literacy/ICTwhitepaperfinal.pdf

31. Gallup. (2011). The State of the global workplace. Retrieved on December 17, 2011 from http://www.google.com/url?sa=t&rct=j&q=&esrc=s&source=web&cd=2&ved=0CCwQFjAB&url=http://www.gallup.com%2Ffile%2Fconsulting%2F145535%2FState_of_the_Global_Workplace_2011.pdf

32. Gibbard, A. (1994). Meaning and normativity, *Philosophical Issues, 5,* 95-115.

33. Gibson, J.J. (1977). The Theory of affordances. In *Perceiving, Acting, and Knowing,* Eds. Robert Shaw and John Bransford.

34. Gross, B.M. (1962). Operation basic: The Retrieval of wasted knowledge, *Journal of Communication, 12*(2), 67–83.

35. Hamel, G. (2009). Moon shots for management, *Harvard Business Review.* (Reprint 0902H)

36. Hastings, R. (2011) An explanation and some reflections, *Netflix Blog.* Retrieved on November 1, 2011 from http://blog.netflix.com/2011/09/explanation-and-some-reflections.html

37. Heim, A. (2011). Meet the Chilean teen who warns of earthquakes on Twitter, *The Next Web Latin America.* Retrieved on July 18, 2011 at http://thenextweb.com/la/2011/07/18/meet-the-chilean-teen-who-warns-of-earthquakes-on-twitter

38. Hock, D. W., and International, V. (2000). *Birth of the chaordic age.* Berrett-Koehler Publishers.

39. How to dial your phone by Bell System (1954) *YouTube* (video). Retrieved on December 14, 2011 from http://www.youtube.com/watch?v=PuYPOC-gCGA

40. IBM. (2011). Capitalizing on complexity, *Executive, Global Chief, and Officer Study.* (2011).

41. Jenkins, H. (2006). Confronting the challenges of participatory culture: Media education for the 21st century, white paper for *MacArthur Foundation.*

42. Johnson, S. (1999). *Interface culture: How new technology transforms the way we create and communicate.* Basic Books.

43. Jones, B.D. (2001). *Politics and the architecture of choice: Bounded rationality and governance.* University of Chicago Press.

44. Kaplan, R.S., and Norton, D.P. (2004). *Strategy maps: Converting intangible assets into tangible outcomes.* Harvard Business Press.

45. Koschmann, T., Kuuti, K., & Hickman, L. (1998). The Concept of breakdown in Heidegger, Leont'ev, and Dewey and its implications for education. *Mind, Culture & Activity,* 5(1), 25-41.

46. Kraut, R., Kiesler, S., Boneva, B., Cummings, J., Helgeson, V., and Crawford, A. (2002). Internet paradox revisited *Journal of Social Issues, 58,* 49–74.

47. Kujath, C.L. (2001). Facebook and MySpace: Complement or substitute for face-to-face interaction? *Cyberpsychology, behavior and social networking, 14*(1-2), 75-78.

48. Kuntsche, E., et al. (2009). Electronic media communication with friends from 2002 to 2006 and links to face-to-face contacts in adolescence: an HBSC study in 31 European and North American countries and regions. *International journal of public health, 54*(0), 243-50.

49. Lankshear, C., and Knobel, M. (2008). *Digital literacies: concepts, policies and practices.* Vol. 30. Peter Lang Pub Inc.

50. Lankshear, C., and Knobel, M. (2006). *New literacies: Everyday practices and classroom learning*. Open Univ Press.

51. Li, C. (2010). *Open leadership: how social technology can transform the way you lead*. Vol. 167. Jossey-Bass.

52. Manovich, L. (2001). *The language of new media*. The MIT press.

53. McAfee, A. (2009). *Enterprise 2.0: New collaborative tools for your organization's toughest challenges*. Harvard Business School Press.

54. McLuhan, M. (2003). *Understanding Media,* critical ed. Corte Madera: Gingko Press

55. McLuhan, M., and McLuhan, E. (1988). *Laws of Media. The New Science*. Toronto and Buffalo: University of Toronto Press.

56. Mintzberg, H. (1979) *The Structuring of organizations,* Englewood Cliffs, NJ:Prentice-Hall.

57. Morrissey, B. (2010). Wieden Hires Poke's Iain Tait for Digital, *AdWeek*. Retrieved on 12/12/11 from http://www.adweek.com/news/advertising-branding/wieden-hires-pokes-iain-tait-digital-101480.

58. Old Spice Channel, YouTube. http://www.youtube.com/oldspice#p/c/484F058C3EAF7FA6

59. Ostrom, E. (2005). *Understanding institutional diversity*. Princeton University Press.

60. Ostrom, E. (2011). Background on the institutional analysis, *Policy Studies, 39*(1), 7-27.

61. Papert, S. (1987). *A critique of technocentrism in thinking about the school of the future*. Retrieved September 15, 2011 from http://www.papert.org/articles/ACritiqueofTechnocentrism.html

62. Papert, S., and Resnick, M. (1995). *Technological fluency and the representation of knowledge*. Proposal to the National Science Foundation. MIT Media Laboratory.

63. Parpis, E. (2010). Spice It Up, *Adweek*. Retrieved on July 26, 2010 from http://www.adweek.com/news/advertising-branding/spice-it-102895

64. Parr, B. (2009). How two roommates saved a dog's life using Twitter, *Mashable*. Retrieved on May 24, 2009 at http://mashable.com/2009/05/24/twitter-dog

65. Pettit, T. (2007). Before the Gutenberg Parenthesis: Elizabethan-American compatibilities, at *MIT5 Conference*. http://web.mit.edu/comm-forum/mit5/papers/pettitt_plenary_gutenberg.pdf

66. Pollet, T.V., Roberts, S.G.B., and Dunbar, R.I.M. (2011). Use of social network sites and instant messaging does not lead to increased offline social network size, or to emotionally closer relationships with offline network members, *Cyberpsychology, behavior and social networking 14*(4), 253- 258.

67. Ramaswamy, V. and Gouillart, F. (2010). *The Power of Co-Creation: Build It with Them to Boost Growth, Productivity and Profits*. New York: Free Press.

68. Resnick, M. (2002). Rethinking learning in the digital age. In G. Kirkman (Ed.), *The global information technology report: Readiness for the networked world*. Oxford, UK: Oxford University Press.

69. Richard, J.S. (1997). The Learning Army, approaching the 21st century as a learning organization. Retrieved on September 28, 2011 from http://oai.dtic.mil/oai/oai?verb =getRecord&metadataPrefix=html&identifier=ADA327188

70. Schön, D.A. (1971). *Beyond the stable state*. Random House New York.

71. Schon, D A. (1983). *The Reflective Practitioner: How Professionals Think in Action*. Basic Books.

72. Segall, L. (2011) Boozy Red Cross tweet turns into marketing bonanza for Dogfish Brewery, *CNN Money*. Retrieved on December 16, 2011 from http://money.cnn. com/2011/02/17/smallbusiness/dogfish_redcross/index.htm

73. Senge, P. (1998). Sharing Knowledge, *Society for Organizational Learning*. Retrieved on March 20, 2012 from http://www.solonline.org/res/kr/shareknow.html

74. Shirky, C. (2008). *Here comes everybody: the power of organizing without organizations*. Penguin Press.

75. Simon, H.A. (1973). Applying to information technology design organization, *Public Administration Review, 33*(3), 268-278.

76. Smith, P. (2010) The Twitchhiker: The amazing story of how Paul Smith travelled the world for free using only Twitter, *Mail Online*. Retrieved on July 11, 2010 from http://www.dailymail.co.uk/news/article-1293636/The-Twitchhiker-The-amazing-story-Paul-Smith-travelled-world-free-using-Twitter.html

77. Spira, J.B. (2011). *Overload!: How Too Much Information is Hazardous to Your Organization*. Wiley.

78. Stiehm, J.H., and Townsend, N.W. (2002). *The U.S. Army War College: Military Education in a Democracy*. Temple University Press.

79. Tocqueville, A. (1835). *Democracy in America*.

80. Toffler, A. (1970). Future shock, *Amereon Ltd., New York*.

81. Uexküll, J. (1920). *Kompositionslehre der Natur*. (Edited by Thure von Uexküll). Frankfurt am Main.

82. US Army FM 5-0 Field Operations Manual. (2010). Retrieved on December 17, 2011 from http://www.fas.org/irp/doddir/army/fm5-0.pdf

83. Vermeulen, F. (2011). So, you think you have a strategy? *London Business School Business Strategy Review*. Retrieved on December 17, 2011 from http://bsr.london. edu/lbs-article/629/index.html

84. von Hippel, E. (1986) Lead users: A source of novel product concepts, *Management Science, 32*(7), 791-805.

85. Wasserman, T. (2009). Skittles wikis its home page, *Adweek*. Retrieved on February 27, 2009 from http://www.adweek.com/news/technology/skittles-wikis-its-home-page-98536

86. Wellman, B., Haase, A. Q., Witte, J., and Hampton, K. (2001). Does the Internet increase, decrease, or supplement social capital? Social networks, participation, and community commitment. *American Behavioral Scientist, 45* (3), 436-455.

87. Wiancko, R. (2010). And the 'Oldspice Maneuver' is created, blows the doors off of advertising, *The Blog of* रायन. Retrieved on July 15, 2010 from http://ryanwiancko.com/2010/07/15/and-the-oldspice-maneuver-is-created-blows-the-doors-off-of-advertising

88. World Without Oil. http://worldwithoutoil.org/metaabout.htm

89. Worsham, S. (2010). Measurable effects of Old Spice viral campaign, *Sazbean*. Retrieved on July 15, 2010 from http://sazbean.com/2010/07/15/measurable-effects-of-old-spice-viral-campaign

90. Zaidi, A. (2010). Is it too early to analyse ROI from the Old Spice campaign?, *Econsultancy Digital Marketers United*. Retrieved on July 23, 2010 from http://econsultancy.com/us/blog/6305-is-it-too-early-to-analyse-roi-from-the-old-spice-campaign

91. Zhao S. (2006). Do internet users have more social tie? A call for differentiated analyses of internet use. *Journal of Computer-Mediated Communication, 11*, 844–62.

About the Authors

Christian Briggs

Christian Briggs is working on a Ph.D. in Human-Computer Interaction and Complex Systems at the Indiana University School of Informatics and Computing, where he occasionally teaches courses in new media theory. His research focuses primarily on how people get things done in organizations using digital technology together. Christian previously worked in various creative, management and consultative roles for Palladium Group, Ziff Davis Interactive, Surfwatch, Walt Disney Imagineering, One to One Interactive and Walmart. Christian co-founded SociaLens in 2009 to provide research, training and consulting to help organizations to thrive in the digital age.

Kevin Makice

Kevin Makice is a co-founder of SociaLens and a Ph.D. candidate at the Indiana University School of Informatics and Computing. His past research is eclectic, including political wikis, tangible interfaces for children's games, machinima, and network analysis of ball movement in basketball. In 2009, Kevin authored the first technical book about Twitter, *Twitter API: Up and Running*, published by O'Reilly Media. Kevin is a contributor to *Wired*'s GeekDad blog.

Larry Buchanan

Larry Buchanan is a freelance illustrator and designer. He graduated from Indiana University in 2011 with a degree in journalism and a concentration in fine art. While in school, Buchanan was named student designer of the year by the Society of News Design and Indiana Collegiate Journalist of the Year by the Indiana Collegiate Press Association. He illustrates a bi-weekly visual column for McSweeney's Internet Tendency about being a recent college graduate and still living in a college town. He lives in a little log cabin in just south of IU's campus with his wife Erin (who copy edited this book) and their dog and cat.

Want to find out how digitally fluent you are?

Take a short survey at mydigitalfluency.socialens.com to find out.

Also, you can connect with us to keep up with our ongoing research, share stories of your journey to digital fluency, or ask questions here:

Twitter: @SociaLens
Facebook: facebook.com/SociaLens
Web: SociaLens.com

Made in the USA
Middletown, DE
23 January 2018